Stevie Davies is ow .e ..., . . .y of Literature and the Welsh Academy, and Director of Creative Writing at Swansea University. Her previous titles include *Four Dreamers and Em , v, Impassioned Clay* and *The Element of Wa ',* which was longlisted for the Booker and Orange Prizes and won the Arts Council of Wales Aw 1. Her latest novel, *Kith and Kin,* is also available n Phoenix paperback.

The Web of Belonging

STEVIE DAVIES

PHOENIX

A PHOENIX PAPERBACK

First published in Great Britain in 1997
by The Women's Press
This paperback edition published in 2004
by Phoenix,
an imprint of Orion Books Ltd,
Orion House, 5 Upper St Martin's Lane,
London WC2H 9EA

A CIP catalogue record for this book
is available from the British Library.

ISBN 0 75381 908 2

Printed and bound in Great Britain by
Clays Ltd, St Ives plc

0298860⁹

To Alan Plater and
Shirley Rubinstein
With love

AUTHOR'S ACKNOWLEDGEMENTS

I gratefully acknowledge the Arts Council Writer's Award which supported the writing of this novel. And I thank my literary agent, Jane Bradish-Ellames of Curtis Brown, for all she has given.

When female virtue weds with manly worth,
We catch the rapture and we spread it forth.

(Inscription on bell number 4 of the 12 bells of St Chad's Church, Shrewsbury)

CHAPTER 1

'Come on, love,' I said to Jacob. 'Let's saunter. When did we last amble? We're always on the gallop – especially you, poor love.'

'Can we even remember how to do it?' He smiled and shrugged.

A woman was lounging on a bench on Pride Hill, hands loose on her lap, palm-upward as if cupped to catch the milky stream of early April, late afternoon warmth. Tall and rangy, with brown shoulder-length hair and round glasses, she wore a backpack from which an ordnance survey map showed. Her eyes browsed us with the air of a bystander, freely looking on, disengaged from the medium in which we were embroiled.

'I bet she knows how to saunter,' I murmured.

She did. Giving me a shy smile, she turned and trailed her shadow up the brick mosaic of the pedestrian area, into McDonald's.

'Who?' Jacob asked.

'Oh, she's gone now.'

We sauntered as best we could, into the Square, where we sat under the statue of Clive of India, with the sun on our backs.

'This is so lovely,' I observed. It was still, after twenty years, so special to be out anywhere with Jacob. Two decades of tenderness welled up. I reached for his hand

and asked what he was thinking. He seemed absorbed in some private thoughts, far-away or idle.

'Oh, nothing much, Jessie,' he said mildly, but did he sigh at feeling called to account? 'I'm enjoying the peace – and the air. Just generally being off-duty.'

I let be, never wanting to pester: I've always shrunk from invading the personal space that is rightfully closed to outsiders, even to the companion of one's life. The Quakers have always seemed so right about the inner light of each person, the need to respect it. That shining impromptu sabbath: I see it now on a screen, like the closure of a film.

It was banal, beautiful; an interlude plucked from our routine of drudging obligations. I remember that I avoided the eye of the clock on the Market Building. I didn't want to remember the Oldies. The Oldies were being baby-sat by Hannah Roberts so that we could have an afternoon off. They like Hannah: even Jacob's mum likes Hannah. *She takes me seriously*, said May jutting her jaw at me. *Not like some I could mention*.

May's voice, bless her, can get into your mind and drown out your own. I remember consciously having to switch off her transmission as the black-and-white clock on the Market Building reminded me that all sabbath afternoons must come to an end.

And so we basked at Clive's foot (stuck out over the plinth as if poised to step down and colonise us from the past), and Jacob sprawled his six foot length, throwing his arms out along the back of the bench and leaning his head back with an uninhibited yawn.

Pigeons strutted amongst pebble-dashed flowerpots, the sun picking out the pink of their legs and feet, the surprising orange of their eyes. Two albinos ranged amongst them, a purer white than any dove, each foraging bird travelling with a long and busy shadow.

The Sunday families strolled, smiled, lolled.

'I could stay here forever,' I said. An irreverent sparrow perched on Clive's head, mocking the greenly tarnished hero's swagger.

'Look,' I said. 'There's that woman again.'

'Which woman?'

'The one with the ordnance survey map.'

Jacob looked vaguely up as the tall woman passed us by and seated herself at the next bench.

'What are you so interested in her for?' he asked me. 'She looks perfectly ordinary to me. Downright plain.'

I was conscious of blenching. He has never been in the habit of talking of women in that way.

Plainer than me? The question darted through my mind. I pulled my skirt down over my knees which seemed bulbous. I felt fat and dowdy.

'She looks . . . free,' I said.

A swift, startled look from Jacob: 'Envious?'

Goodness, no. I'd enjoyed a more fulfilled life than anyone I've ever known. I had the twenty-year love of a husband I adored; people to care for who valued me; the fellowship of the church; deep roots in Shrewsbury. There are not many people lucky enough to have inherited the house where they were born, a beautiful house too, in Kingsland, overlooking the river. Open house for folk in need of succour, that's how I justify to myself our plenty. Only children have eluded us. We did have Nella, our darling Nella whom we fostered – but her mother took her back; and that may have been right for Nella, though I wonder? I often wonder.

No: that woman intrigued me not because I envied her apparently floating status as an onlooker but because of the gentle attentiveness with which she was making her stationary appraisal. This you can only do if you are not embroiled.

'Well, go and chat to her if she interests you so much. She can be one of your stray lambs.'

'Oh, Jacob.'

'Only teasing, love. Go on. I bet she's got a husband and six children at home, waiting for their tea. Go and find out.'

He gave another extravagant yawn.

Why did he yawn so much that afternoon? Was he bored? tired? not feeling himself? Was it the sleepiness of the sun? That week he'd been opening up her attic for Mrs McKillop in Monkmoor, all on his own. It took him ten days working flat-out, without aid of any sort except for Jamie Tyrer helping to carry up the hardboard. He's a wonderful workman, of the old school, taking a pride in doing the job well, undercharging according to means. There aren't many Jacobs left: carpenters, not joiners.

'You have the most superior McDonald's I've ever been in,' said the travelling woman, with a light laugh. 'So genteel. Endless mopping of floors and window-cleaning! Oh, it's such a gentle place, Shrewsbury,' she went on with the breathless eagerness that begs you not to dispute her intuition that the pebble she has come across is really a pearl. 'So civilised. So unlike Manchester!'

'A lot has been ruined,' I said. 'Even in my time. And we have a problem of homelessness here too – and drugs – and vandals.'

Desecration is in the air. Only this week vandals stole a thousand plaques from a cemetery. A thousand plaques. A thousand names effaced.

'But you still have such a caring community,' she pleaded. 'I can feel it.'

'Well – we've had education axed, a hundred-odd teachers sacked – and homes for the elderly closed; eight more to be privatised next year – and twelve million cut from next year's budget...'

'But I've never seen so many charity shops in my whole life! Every other shop's a charity shop...' Crestfallen, she was evidently hanging on to the determination that we should be nothing like Manchester. She gestured over to the black-and-white Tudor house erected by Richard Owen, Gent., several hundred years ago. 'And such beautiful architecture,' she insisted. 'And you have Park-and-Ride schemes, I've seen the coaches.'

'Yes, yes, we do,' I conceded. I did not add that the whole town is under threat from traffic pollution; asthma is soaring. I bit back the sharp retort that would bereave a wistful nomad of her dream. 'There is still a community spirit here, and so many good people. And look at the plus side, we've got the tallest Town Crier in the world, he's seven foot two.'

'Ah, but what's his voice like?'

'Loud.'

She giggled.

'And how about you – I gather you come from Manchester?'

And, yes, she was Mancunian, and free, as I'd thought, with all the ambivalence of freedom; just divorced, apparently, and on her own; drifting for a while, quit of obligation, looking on. We chatted and I warmed to her, wishing her Godspeed.

When I turned back to Jacob, he was gone.

And this is why I am remembering that perfectly ordinary Sunday afternoon. When I turned round, he was gone. A cloud over the sun cast us all in shadow; and the spasms of traffic noise paused. I looked round and he wasn't there. Oh, but there he was, near the door of Waterstone's, the windows full of Ellis Peters books;

talking to some woman I divined only as a flash of ash-blonde hair. She vanished into Waterstones.

'Who was that?' I asked.

'Oh – no one in particular, Jessie love. She thought she knew me.'

Affectionate then, he kissed me full on the lips; and I was blissfully proud of my tall, distinguished husband as we sauntered down Mardol Head into the sun; passed our Baptist chapel and entered the narrow shut of Claremont Hill on our way to the Quarry.

'Well, at least the Council hasn't managed to spoil this,' Jacob said, as we relished the russet elegance of the Georgian terrace. 'With their crack-brained schemes.'

'They're trying,' I said. 'You can't expect them to get round to it all at once. That woman . . .'

'Which woman?' he blurted.

'The woman I was talking to just now.'

'Oh, that woman.'

'She was saying how unspoiled it is here.'

'Ah.'

'We must come out more often, Jacob,' I said, as we ambled down to the Dingle in rushing wind and sunlight, the Quarry avenues of limes tender-green with the season's new leaves.

He returned no answer. He looked thoughtful.

'Don't you think, love?' I pursued.

'Surely.' Jacob's attention seemed to have drifted away again.

'It's not that I begrudge the Oldies our time: not in any way: please don't think that. I love them dearly.'

'Of course you do.'

Of course I do.

'Oh,' said May. 'Look what the wind's blown in. My

oh my. Fancy you two deigning to come home. We might have died and you wouldn't have known.'

'But you had Hannah with you, darling,' I said. 'You were quite safe. And we were only out for three hours.'

Hannah said they'd had a lovely time watching the golf and sewing squares of knitting together for an Oxfam blanket. Well, she had done the sewing and May and Brenda had advised. Brenda had talked her into joining the Woodland Trust: together they would sponsor a copse and save the ... she couldn't remember ... 'What are we saving again, Brenda?'

Brenda, May's sister, an ex-geography teacher who belongs to a number of societies and guilds, promptly reminded her, 'Oak, beech and ancient hornbeam – habitat for the dormouse, the nightingale and various butterflies including the silver-washed fritillary.'

'That's right,' said easy-going Hannah. 'That's what we're going to save.'

'In the last fifty years half of Britain's ancient forest has been destroyed,' stated Brenda, reaffirming a point she had made at length over breakfast. 'It's wickedness.'

This statement put May in a worse pet, for she considers herself to have a monopoly of Green causes, and resents what she regards as attempted take-overs. 'Frigging fritillaries,' she growsed; and we ignored her language.

'Yes,' went on Brenda, 'you can be a Woodland Planter, a Woodland Guardian or a Woodland Benefactor.'

'Which one did I say I'd be?' asked Hannah.

'A Benefactor. You will have five trees planted for you every year. Your trees, your very own. And when you die, they'll still be there.'

'When I die, sling my ashes off the Stiperstones,' said May. 'By the Devil's Chair. And it can't be soon enough,' she added, mentioning the coming Friday as a possible date.

'Now now,' said Hannah, 'we'll have you with us for years yet, May, keeping us in order;' and she began to collect together her things, in her usual sweetly scatty way. Nathan, she thought, had been engaged in private Bible-study in his room. May snorted atheistically. Hannah departed mildly pointing out to anyone who was listening that she was so glad that Jacob and I had enjoyed a lovely afternoon together; we needed an occasional break.

This was not what Jacob's mother wanted to hear.

'Oh,' she flounced, a storm gathering, 'she thinks she's so wonderful, does that Dee Dee . . .'

I still wonder why she called me Dee Dee: it's nothing like my name. My friend Catherine, who has done a Social Anthropology course at Shrewsbury College, says that some tribes rename members if they seem threatening, to assert power over them. 'It must be that poor May feels so helpless,' said Catherine. 'And you're her life-line.'

Catherine is wise and so gentle: if only we could be more together, but I have the Oldies and she is pretty well tied with a family of youngsters. Still, there is always the phone.

May was fuming on.

'But let me tell you, young woman, that there's a lady in Meole Brace who has been looking after six priests for forty-five years who's been given a medal by the Pope. Yes, it's true, it's in the *Star*. Oh, you don't believe me, I see, Dee Dee. Brenda, pass *The Shropshire Star* so I can show her. See? Six priests. Six is a hell of a lot of priests, and all probably fussy eaters.'

Sure enough, a presbytery housekeeper in Meole Brace had been thus honoured by the Holy See.

'I'll toddle,' said Jacob, who'd been hovering in the background: off for a slow pint at his local, The Crown, where he sits in his quiet, calm way on the Riverside Terrace, making it last and watching the river flow by.

'Right, love. See you soon.' The front door clicked behind him. He was gone.

'See!' shrieked May. 'See! He's hardly in the door than he wants out again. And you think you're the bees' knees and paramount! You don't even stay in and look after us properly. You'll get no medals from me, I'm telling you.'

'But sweetheart,' I said, crouching down beside her, kissing her soft cheek. 'I don't think it's in the least bit virtuous to look after you – I like sharing your lives – it's what I want to do.'

'So what do you keep going out for, if you like it so much?'

I am their wall; their rock.

Jacob is my wall; my rock. I have not encountered the solidity of this truth until now. Jacob was there, a quality of my being; a rootedness, a quiet.

We have taken in his relatives one by one as they became helpless and dependent. It seemed the natural thing to do, since we had the necessary space and with my parents dead and Nella gone. When May joined us, I relinquished my job at the Castle Gates Library. For though Aunt Brenda was frail and nervous, she could safely be left during the day provided someone popped in at lunchtime; but May, never the easiest of women, has become turbulent, and needs constant watching and careful handling. She punched the health visitor full on the jaw because she disliked her face and officious manners.

'Well, I didn't like her face either, May, but I did not

view that as a reason for punching her,' Brenda lucidly objected.

'Barging in like that. What did she expect?'

Somewhat after that, Jacob's elderly cousin Nathan also joined us. Nathan, who is of a holy disposition, was shocked by May's retributive violence. He quoted Scripture at her and, when she stormed at him, retired to his room promising to pray for her. Nathan is no obvious trouble at all, keeping mainly to his room, where I serve his meals on a tray. Nathan is almost too grateful for the little things I do for him.

But his piety inflames May. When he withdrew to pray for her, she fumed against the Holy Ghost and flailed her stick.

Eighteen months ago the taking-in of Nathan seemed the right course of action but no longer the natural one. I sucked in my breath, conscious of a strain, an inner reluctance which must be overcome. I turned my face fractionally away from my husband's as I assented.

'I'm not sure this is a very good idea. Can you honestly manage, Jess?' Jacob asked concernedly.

'Of course I can. Yes . . . of course.'

'I think it's too much for you, love. I do, really.'

He took my shoulders between those large, kind hands; looked down with apology in his pale eyes. Then as at the beginning there was nothing, nothing, I would not do for Jacob. He too appeared worn, as if the life were being slowly ground out of him.

'But what about you, love? You get no home life to speak of.'

No sooner was Jacob seated in the evening than his mother besieged him, her voice swooping and stabbing in a state of frenetic arousal. He had become quiet and withdrawn. But it was not in his nature to complain.

He stayed out longer and longer on the job, often not coming home until long after the Oldies were in bed.

'Well but I get respite during the day, don't I? You have all the graft. And I feel guilty really because they're my relatives.'

'Our relatives, Jacob. Ours. I can manage fine. And Nathan will not be a burden in the same way as ... I mean, he's a nice, inoffensive man. I'd rather *not* see him go to a home.'

'If you're sure. . . .'

'I think it's maybe our duty. Since we have the room to spare – and I'm at home anyway.'

If I hadn't predicted the stimulus Nathan's godliness would be to May, that was because he made sure never to parade it. Like Christ he was humble and tolerant; but like Christ's his gentle conviction generated its own eloquence and its own conspicuousness.

'There's a nasty smell in here,' stated May on Nathan's first day with us. Having unpacked his suitcase and stowed away his austere possessions, I helped Nathan to an armchair drawn up in the circle before the gas fire and denominated his.

'I can't smell one,' said Brenda.

'There's no bad smell, Mother, truly,' I insisted.

'Yes there is. Can't you smell it, Brenda? Can't you really? Ugh. Pass me a peg, Jess, I want to peg my nose.'

Gently I chafed her hand, understanding her disquiet at the kerfuffle attendant on the arrival of a new resident. 'All is well, Mother,' I reassured her. 'Be calm now, dear, do. All's well, I promise you.'

'But the stink!' she burst out. 'The frightful pong! You know what it is, don't you?' She beckoned down my face, whispering conspiratorially but quite audibly, 'It wasn't here before he came and it won't be here after he's gone.'

Nathan rearranged his narrow, nervous limbs in his chair. The move had fatigued him, together with the trauma of leaving the little house in Frankwell where he had lived with his beloved Bethan until her death last year. Nathan had much grieving yet to do. Closing his eyes, he murmured to himself, no doubt in prayer.

'May – don't.' I pulled away, scolding. 'That's hurtful – and so untrue.' I pointed out that Nathan was a tidy, wholesome and well-washed person.

'Oh,' said May, 'I didn't mean Body Odour, Jess. What do you think I am – nesh? When you've been brought up on a farm amongst all the manure you don't worry about earthly stink. Agriculture is in my veins. I'm talking about the odour of Righteousness. Horrible.' She screwed her features into a grimace.

'Don't worry, Jess,' said Nathan. 'I'm not upset.'

'He's not upset,' echoed Brenda in relief.

'Damned smelly hypocrite,' muttered May. 'Thank Christ all the churches are being given over to the Redundant Churches Fund or turned into Building Societies. Soon there won't be one open at all in Shrewsbury, Nathaniel Banana, and then where will you be?'

'If you mean St Mary's, May dear,' said Nathan with gentle restraint, 'I'm not C of E, so it doesn't affect me. And, you know, any place where two or three are gathered together in Jesu's name can count as a sacred place – even a private house.'

'Oh yes, even a lavatory, I suppose,' jeered May, inflamed and itching to inflame others.

'In the last resort . . .' he paused, appearing to wrestle for an answer at once accurate and pacifying, ' . . . that may be. But how lovely the mimosa is in your garden,' said Nathan. 'I've been admiring it.'

'Jessie is a wonderful gardener. She has green fingers,' said Brenda proudly.

'Jess, from what I can see, is a wonderful everything.'

'Filthy stinker, thinks he's a damned saint,' said May, but quietly, as an internal memorandum. I hoped she was subsiding and that Nathan, with a normal ration of septuagenarian deafness, had not heard.

I handed the three their tea, which was eagerly consumed. Brenda dunked her biscuits and sucked at them pleasurably, speaking of the Lace Fair at Harlescott, which she hoped to attend with Peter Fox, our dear friend from church and the only male member of the local Guild of Lacemakers. When May nodded off shortly after the beginning of this discourse, I hoped that when she awoke she'd have forgotten the suspicious smell. But no. It was worse than ever.

For some time, Nathan took his cue from me and ignored her insults. But presently (and I could hardly blame him) he began to retaliate by forgiving her; blatantly turning the other cheek and conferring unwelcome blessings. The more she cursed, the more he blessed, his Christian spirit galling May to the point where she could contemplate little but her wrongs. May flung things at his wall and shouted at it in his stead. Her parents had been strict Baptists from whose codes senility had released her to riot and mayhem. Perhaps, Jacob and I speculated, she imagined the repressive parents behind that wall: Nathan had a speaking facial resemblance to her father. Certainly after Nathan's coming she became not only uncontrollable but a malign spirit dedicated to the destruction of all household peace.

'I could always go into a home,' Nathan offered.

'This is your home, Nathan,' I replied promptly. 'May will just have to get used to that.'

'I do pray for her.'

'Of course you do.'

'And please let me help with tasks such as the dusting. It will be slow but I am quite capable of it.'

Why Nathan's dusting activities should have exacerbated my temper more than all May's tantrums put together has never been fully clear to me. It was so carefully done. Grasping the edge of the sideboard with one brittle hand, he would tremblingly wipe with the other. He made scarcely any fuss; consciously solicited no attention.

But the dusting has always been my favourite work. I do it methodically, raising in sequence each ornament or picture, recognising it as mine – ours – replacing it in the exactly right spot. Order brings reassurance. As I move steadily round each room, retracing my steps of yesterday, my inner space is composed until a random scatter achieves a geometry at once complex and humanly warm.

Nathan's helpfulness, which I cannot bring myself to reject, generates an unease I can neither rectify nor justify.

'Don't trouble yourself. Please.'

'It's no trouble, my dear. I like to help.'

My 'Please' had come out as a faltering supplication, which he omitted to register.

'Nathan, it's unnecessary, you know, I –'

'There's little I can do for you, Jess, to show how much I appreciate . . . but let me just do that. Unless of course,' he added, 'I'm getting in your way?'

'No, of course not.' I should have explained then, but typically could not bring myself to do so.

'Jesus wept!' shrieked May. 'It's the Angel of the Lord with his golden duster. Go and play your harp, holy Joe. You're just a bally nuisance. Nought but a nuisance. Isn't he, Jess?'

'No, of course not, May, he's a . . .' I drew in a deep breath, 'great help.'

'Oh, you're always on *his* side,' she sulked. 'I can't say a word right. It's always *him* that's your darling.' She scratched at the peeling skin of her wrists, where the dermatitis is so red-raw it seems to turn her inside-out. Though she suffers a good deal of pain, she rarely complains directly. Her old mottled face began to crumple like a child's.

'You're my darling too,' I soothed, going to her, fondling her hand. 'In a special way.'

'Am I?' Her eyes peeped sidelong.

'Of course you are, of course. You know that.'

'If you say so,' she acquiesced, but then her shoulders drooped. 'We were happy till *he* came, and why you didn't put him in a home, Jessica, I shall never know – he could have been more persecuted there, and reviled and stoned like St What's-is-name in the desert. He likes that, the stinking little martyr.'

'St Stephen?' suggested Nathan. 'But I don't set up for a saint, May. I'm a common sinner the Lord has touched with his saving breath.' He dusted the lamp-stand conscientiously.

'Hallelujah.'

'Can't you just . . . accept him darling?' I asked May.

'You don't care about me no more now you've got him.' Her head sank to her collar.

'Well, you're still my darling whatever you say,' I chirruped, brightly, crisply. When I rose to my feet, my back caught and my eyes locked in to the eyes in the mirror. A blank dread was in that brown stare. A door seemed to swing open on noiseless hinges; to swing open and not to close, but to revolve forever round a pointless point – a door you could never go through.

What was it for then, the door, if you could never go through it?

Occasionally this happens when I am fatigued, this uncanny sense of dreaming awake. Something is wrong. But what? I quiver from head to foot, unnerved.

Brenda spasmed with fright. She watched me intently for signs of crumbling.

'What's the matter, what's the matter?'

'Oh – nothing, love. Bit of backache, that's all.'

'Sit down now, do sit down,' she fussed. 'You overdo it. Leave her be, May, don't be so selfish. What would you do if she collapsed?'

'Die,' said May categorically. 'Die and rot and be eaten by maggots.' She pronounced this doom with a certain ghastly relish.

I sat at the morning-room table and shook, staring out at the olive-green river. The Severn flows past the end of our lush and sloping garden, so that we inhabit a little Shropshire Venice but fresher and more rural. Steepening terraces shelve to the river bank, and a little jetty where Jacob's rowing boat is moored. Before my parents died and his relatives came, in that golden interlude with Nella, we'd bask the summer long in a hedged recess of the lawn with pots of tea, while crews from Shrewsbury School skulled downriver and upriver, the masters pedalling along the towpath, bawling orders through loud-hailers. Along the opposite shore strides a line of aslant limes, beneath which stroll mothers with pushchairs, pensioners, joggers. It seems perpetual sabbath over there. Indeed, the sabbath has retired to the far bank.

CHAPTER 2

'What did he say when he left?' asks Catherine. She has her youngest child with her, a dead weight of rosy boyhood asleep against her shoulder. Every so often she lugs him up from where he sags.

'He just said *I'll toddle.*'

'Well, that doesn't sound very dramatic.'

'No – no, it doesn't. It's what he always says when he goes to the pub.'

Catherine and I sit baffled in the bay window, staring at one another, unable to imagine a man leaving wife, mother, aunt and cousin with the banal words *I'll toddle*, and heading his van to Calais or off a cliff.

'He must have had an . . . accident.'

'But if he had, the police would have been in touch – surely? I shouldn't worry,' says Catherine uneasily.

That evening had become progressively less harassing as it unfolded. Once May had got over the affront of Jacob's and my joint three-hour defection, her spirits rose, as a result of Nathan's departure for evening service with a group of Methodist friends in their minibus.

Having compared the odour of his holiness with the notorious smell at Snailbeach lead mines, made from dried sewage sludge and marketed by Wessex Water in the name of purification, she abseiled from Nathan to

Snailbeach, from Snailbeach to snails and beaches, from beaches to beeches, and thence descended into contemplative quiet over her six o'clock cup of tea.

She welcomed Peter Fox and Brenda's friend Tisha when they arrived, like the most genial old lady on the face of the earth.

I left them to it and spent half an hour in the garden drifting about in the scent of broom and hawthorn, watching the pewter river tarnish as the sun dropped behind the blackness of the yew hedge. I noted the tokens of spring and thought back over the lazy blessings of the day.

We must enjoy many more such days, I thought. For one thing, I owe it to Jacob – and, for another, martyrdom is *not* a virtue.

'Aren't you chilly out here?' asked Peter. Such a nice man; never married but always so fond of me, I've often had to repress irritation as he pads after me from room to room. Not very liberal: looks grave when told that Jacob is in the pub. He doesn't say aloud, but one can't fail to hear it, *On a Sunday?*

'Not a bit.'

I'd been snared: I sighed and followed him indoors, where Tisha was expounding to Brenda the latest on the mammoth bones found in Condover Quarry. Brenda was in a fit of palaeontological excitement which made her for the duration entirely oblivious to the pain from her osteoporosis, which tends to peak in the evenings and generally sends her to bed by eight. I wince for the anguish she so stoically bears, and blessed the woolly mammoths for overriding it that evening. I perched on the arm of her chair, my arm over the back.

Brenda was all for the idea of setting up a special museum of the Ice Age.

'We should be proud of our mammoths,' she insisted.

'Our mammoths are worth a home of their own. It would be an educational asset too, because, don't forget, children love dinosaurs and big beasties of all kinds.'

Tisha thought we ought to have them in the Music Hall. The Music Hall was central. We could all view the mammoths there, on our way to the shops.

'Councillor Chambers thinks they ought to be at Frankwell,' she said disgustedly. 'The others are hedging. *In Shrewsbury somewhere*, says Councillor Marmion. I ask you. *In Shrewsbury somewhere*. Typical. There we are with the best set of mammoths in the country – perhaps in the world – and nowhere to put them.'

'Well, you see, dear,' said Brenda, 'if you open a Museum of the Ice Age, you can gather in relics from all over the Marches. Such as those ancient mouse-like droppings they found near Ludlow. Now, those droppings are of immense scientific interest, but of course, being such lowly objects and so small, they do not attract the same interest as mammoth bones. But put them *near* the mammoths and people will automatically be drawn to them.'

As she unfolded this cunning plan, Brenda's excitement grew. She beguiled herself with the vision of a world in touch with its venerable roots; a population civilised by geology. I stroked her shoulder gently with my fingertips. It is always so touching to see her come alight; the mind glowing in the ruin of her body.

'Well, I take your point,' said Tisha scrupulously but dubiously. 'But I still think there's a lot to be said for the Music Hall. Anyhow, we'll both probably be dead and buried by the time they decide.'

They could agree about that.

'You two Charlies can be on show with the mammoths,' observed May, in a pleasant tone. 'Stuffed.'

Up the stairs they sailed in the chair-lift, one by one;

May giggling as she invariably does when she's in a good mood at bedtime, saying it's better than the helter-skelter; and vowing that she will go to the fair when it next comes: it's never too late, Dee Dee, to start enjoying yourself after you've wasted seventy years eroding your knee-caps in fruitless prayer.

'Have a go yourself, Dee Dee, and don't be such a sour-puss.'

She insisted I strap myself in and up I came in our homely funicular.

'Now, wasn't that fun?' she hectored.

'It was. It was great fun, Mum.'

'You see, you *can* have fun at home: you don't need to keep gadding and gallivanting off. Go on, have another go. Treat yourself.'

'Well, I won't if you don't mind: Brennie's to come up yet.'

'Spoilsport.' She pouted throughout her wash, refusing to co-operate as I manoeuvred her into bed. It's difficult to know how incapacitated May really is, or needs to be. The physio maintained that she could do a lot more than she does (but she sent him packing); and Nathan has seen her marching around when she thought herself unobserved. I take the view that her helplessness, even if only psychological, is real and must be attended to.

'There you are, my darling,' I said, tucking her in.

Up sailed Brennie, in evident excruciating pain, with absolutely no fuss. I helped her into bed, counting out her pills; tucked her in.

I went down for Nathan, who can manage for himself, and likes to be independent. That too must be respected. He ascended the stairs at his usual careful pace and I hovered listening at the bottom, until I was certain that he was safely in bed.

Peter Fox was still there. But Jacob of course had not returned.

'Jacob not back yet?' he insisted on remarking.

'Not yet. But that's fine. I'm pleased for him to get some relaxation.'

'Oh Jessie, you're such a selfless, coping person. You put us all to shame,' he said.

'No – I'm just cheap and ordinary clay.'

And in the furnace I would crack. I have never seen this before. Our elderly parents seemed and were as proud of my practical dedication to caring for others as of my sister Ellen's career. She became not the physicist of her ambitions but a research pharmacist in Birmingham.

'I make the suppositories, you apply them,' she said. 'There's a logic to it. But how you can endure your life beats me. I honestly couldn't do it. Mary and Martha our mum called us. As I recall, Martha got a lousy deal in the Bible story. Well, I suppose someone has to be Martha.'

Impossible to tell her that I liked my life; loved Jacob; didn't feel I was a Martha, ill-thanked and unregarded.

I concealed my pity for her unballasted life, ditching a husband when he bored her; leaving my nephews with a succession of nannies; living for her work. Pitying, I have also blamed. But this is wrong and I blame myself for blaming.

After my baptism by total immersion, I wanted a life in which I could succour people. I had a pair of hands and people needed hands. There is a ministry, I felt, nearer home than Sri Lanka. Feed my sheep, Jesus said. I baked cakes, pastries, cooked soups and stews; heard people call me wonderful. I confess it has been glorious to be called wonderful.

Yet there is also unease, not only at my sinful pride

in my own paltry works but also because when, after my parents' deaths and Nella's passing, I took in Brenda and May, I did it in good part for myself. And for Jacob; for love of Jacob, binding and bonding me to him, him to me, by rooting ourselves securely in the older generation, since I could not bear his child. I missed the Library, the companionship and intellectual stimulation, but I was fulfilling both a primary urge and a deeper vocation.

It was a troubling compound of sacrifice and selfishness.

Nathan was a duty. I felt in a complicated way better for feeling worse. Nathan gets in my light. His tender spirit overshadows mine. The extra work of tact and management caused by his presence saps my vital energy; I have felt for the first time tested and troubled since he came, thus easing the burden of complacency.

'No, Peter,' I assured him, with entire candour. 'I'm not at all what you imagine. I'm of the earth, earthy.'

And we both laughed. He'd often said I was his idea of an earth-mother. But sometimes, when sharp retorts rise in my throat, as lately they have, I have the uneasy sense of being a blade, sheathed.

'When did you realise he'd not come home?' asks Catherine. 'Oh, do stop squirming, Joe, do.'

It's the mid-morning of a day that already seems to stretch behind us to infinity. Joe is performing twisting and diving actions from Catherine's arms, whose muscles must be burning with the effort to restrain him. Her gentle face shows the stress of attempting to concentrate both on his legitimate craving for action and my need for support. He squirms importantly, his raised eyebrows furrowing his forehead, as if urgent business is calling. Any minute now he will start to bellow.

'At around dawn, I suppose,' I say. 'I half-woke and reached out to the ruck of his half of the quilt, and realised there was no one there. But don't worry, I'm sure he'll come in any minute. It's probably just . . . something that cropped up, and he couldn't get through on the phone.'

Joe is purple in the face. Any minute now he will explode.

Catherine jounces him, rather desperately.

'I'm sure you're right, Jessie love, I do hope so. Have we phoned absolutely everyone?'

Joe explodes.

'Shushy shushy,' pleads Catherine. 'Shushy shushy for Mummy and Auntie Jessie. Be an angel.'

She and I have a friendship at least three decades old; tender and steady, if thinner and less accessible in late years – and I was there to see Davie born, when her husband Alan couldn't make it home from Brussels in time. And there was that strange and never-repeated time when, years ago, we seemed to come so close, before she had the babies and I had the Oldies . . . up there on the hillside, in that autumn sunlight that seemed to gild both of us but was already, in the moment of that kiss, valedictory, retrospective.

'Shushy shushy,' she begs her tiny delinquent, arching his back and hurling himself into space.

'Oh Cathy, thanks for coming. You'd better get back to them now.'

'I better had. Mrs Roberts can only stay an hour. But for Heaven's sake let me know as soon as anything happens.'

'I will, don't worry. Please.'

'Where's Jacob?' asks our aunt as Catherine and Joe depart.

'I honestly don't know,' I murmur, so that May won't hear. 'We're a little bit concerned because he didn't come home last night. But don't worry, dear, I'm sure he's okay.'

Her hands fly up in the air and her thin body flinches. She advises me to look carefully for him, as if a person could go missing in a household like a car-key or a wedding-ring.

'He really isn't here, Brennie.'

'Are his clothes still here?'

'Well, yes, as far as I can tell. Perhaps I'd better have another look.'

Elbowed corduroy jackets, shirts and sweaters swing on their hangers like Oxfam relics of lives vacated: which is where all our clothes originated. We are proud that almost nothing of what we wear is first-hand. Maybe one or two pairs of trousers are missing . . . and the old tweed jacket – or did he throw that away? I pause with my face against the coolness of his shirt and breathe in the absence of his warm body. The Victorian mahogany wardrobe, in which not only my parents' but my grandparents' clothes once hung, smells mothbally, smells of heavy and burdensome pastness.

'He's probably been murdered,' declares May, in dolorous triumph. 'By that mugging gang from the Wrekin.'

'May, for goodness' *sake*,' argues Brenda.

'Of course they're not from the Wrekin originally. They've swept down from Liverpool, marauding as they go. Either that or he's got a floosie. Everyone has floosies nowadays, even parsons have floosies, even Monsignors have their leg over.'

'Shush, May, now stop it. You're upsetting our Jess. Don't you listen to her, Jessie. Not quite right: *you know*.'

'Either that or he's fallen in the river and been drowned like those silly buggers fishing at Quatford.'

Brenda bends forward to pat my hand reassuringly. The index finger of her other hand describes a corkscrew motion at her temples to remind me of how things stand in the head department. 'I think you might perhaps ring the *police*.' She whispers the word *police*.

But May has excellent hearing for her age. 'See, I told you. He's in prison. What did I tell you?'

'I've called them. They're coming round.'

I find that I am unconsciously hugging, rocking myself in my own arms. Brenda looks scared, her narrow shoulders quivering with distress. If Jess fails to hold up their world, what will become of them? The ceiling will founder on their fragile bones, the floor slide away and the cellar be revealed.

'It's really okay, Brennie darling,' I reassure Jacob's aunt. 'We shouldn't worry.'

How many times have I said that this morning: *don't worry*? It's my profession, of course, to say these words; to take upon myself the care that gnaws these souls made frail by age and illness. As the snake-bite healer sucks out the poison, does he ever wonder how long he can continue to function?

'Arrange the funeral,' orders May. 'Ring up Painter's now, Dee Dee. Go on.'

I manage to smile. 'I think it's a bit premature, Mum, to call in the funeral directors when no one's died – don't you?'

She shakes her head; but cannot conceal her relief.

I busy myself with chores, emptying the washing machine, ironing: exuding normality. But as I hum in a breezy way it occurs to me that occasionally he has been really late recently, though he's generally so reliable. Maybe he hasn't cuddled me as much.

I exhort myself not to panic for it is unendurable to think of that darling body, life of my life, washed downstream or clubbed into sudden silence by a hit-and-run driver. I have not comprehended how entirely I depend on Jacob: he was simply there for me, the medium in which I've lived, like light, air, water, bread.

'No! No! Don't ask me! I won't do it!' my mother-in-law squawks when the young policeman is admitted.

'I beg your pardon, madam?'

'I won't come. Someone else will have to go.'

'She thinks you've come to take her to prison,' Brenda explains.

'Of *course* I don't. What do you take me for? A fool?'

'Don't you worry, madam. Nobody's going to take you anywhere.'

'Ah, you say that *now*,' says May with a cunning look. She jabs a rheumatic finger at him. 'But I know you coppers. What's a nice lad like you doing joining the police for anyway? Bursting into the houses of upright citizens. Torturing miners. Beating up those nice vegetarians at Shoreham. *I*'ve seen you. You've been spotted, young man. You've been outed.' She shakes her head and her jowls wobble with the force of her fiercely radical outspokenness.

'May,' I cajole. 'Shush. The policeman's trying to find Jacob. He wants to take down some . . . particulars.'

'Well don't ask *me* to come down to your precious morgue to identify my son's corpse, that's all.'

'There's no body, madam. I'm sure you have no cause for concern.'

I lead the constable through to the morning room where, settling into my father's leather armchair, he assumes a reassuring expression; taps his pencil-end on his notebook. Voices worm through the walky-talky in his breast pocket.

'How old is your husband, Mrs Copplestone?'

'Forty-two – just.'

'When did you last see him? . . . did he seem in any way anxious or agitated? . . . money-problems? . . . had a disagreement? . . . anyone with a grudge? . . . take anything with him?'

'No . . . no . . . no . . . not that I know of.' All my answers are negative. Everything in the house remains normal, commonplace. But my husband has stepped or been dragged or driven over the threshold into an unknown reality, skewing the dimension in which I stand. Nothing holds. Nothing coheres.

'It doesn't make sense,' I repeat.

'He'll most likely turn up. Not to worry.'

'Oh you're going are you?' shrieks May as he passes. 'Off to arrest some poor innocent shoplifter. Arrest the Council if you're looking for criminals. . . . Arrest Shirehall.'

'Quite a character, your mother,' he says appreciatively.

'My husband's mother.'

'Ah.'

'He's nothing like his mother. He's . . . quiet, sober, hard-working.' I paint Jacob duller than he is to protect him from the imputation of May's derangement, keeping private that flighty streak of humour and high spirits that used to have us both dancing in the kitchen, clumping on the lino, laughing till we hurt.

The afternoon shadows' lengths advance and still he has not come. Edgily I concoct reasons for standing tiptoe at the front window and loitering in the garden, within earshot of the phone. Peter finds me at the garden-gate, craning, and I am rather brusque with him.

Catherine arrives and departs. Jane Venner, the pastor's wife rings; and the whole of Shrewsbury seems to be on the telephone reqesting news. Half of Shrewsbury gets short shrift. I am desperate to keep the line open.

May is crying but denies it indignantly.

Nathan, kneeling on a pillow, is petitioning the Lord.

'O merciful Saviour,' his husky voice pleads, 'If it be Thy Holy Will, send our dear Jacob back to us and restore Thine Own lamb to the sheepfold for poor Jess is at her wits' end and even the police know not where he is. But if it be not thy will . . .'

Here he spies me at the door.

' . . . which God forbid, and I am sure, dear Lord, is not thine intention, grant us fortitude to bear these afflictions as did thy servant Job of old. Jess – Jess – ', he pants, attempting to hoist his frail limbs up by hauling on a bookcase with one gnarled hand and pushing on a dressing-table with an elbow, ' – could you give me a hand? I've foolishly – got myself stuck.'

I help him to his feet; he at once topples back on the bed.

'You really shouldn't kneel, you know. Dangerous for you, Nathan. God can see you kneeling in spirit. He doesn't want you to hurt yourself.'

'Ah but – it's a crisis.'

'What if I hadn't been there when you tried to get up and you'd taken a fall?'

'That would have been very selfish of me and put you to great trouble.'

'No, Nathan, I didn't mean that, dear.'

Evening sails down swiftly and softly, like a blue mist from the sky, and exhales from the river in thick breathings on the pane. I prowl the back garden, aware that my anxious presence is disturbing rather than soothing the old people in my care. I've left the back door open, in case the phone rings.

Swans ply by, all sailing east with the tide, the green-brown water pleating in their wakes.

Looking into the evening light, one sees the wet spider's web strung between slats, beaded and glinting with rainbow brilliance, a miracle of engineering as Jacob always says.

The swans return, paddling from above the weir, under the English Bridge, under Greyfriars where twilit children amongst the willows have flung out the last rations of stale bread.

A sighting of May's crazed face at the window haunts me like some reminder of inexplicable guilt. I move beyond its range down the tiers of the garden, wading between ladyfern and a shimmer of dying bluebells.

A single swan rises, its weight of white body low to the water, wings thunder-clapping, beating up spray from the black swan of its shadow.

Jacob's rowing boat remains moored, lapped and rocked by waves. I climb the ladder down into the boat, where I pitch about and finally crouch, my hands on the warm, worn smoothness of the oars.

He may be dead.

He may have had an accident.

He may have lost his memory.

He may have run away and left me to it.

Vestigial sun gilds the ducks and drakes that jab their yellow bills hopefully into the boat.

He can't, my Jacob, he can't, my Jacob can't be gone.

If I don't return to the house there'll be no one to answer the phone or welcome him when he gets back. He'll wonder where I am.

'Where have you been, dear?' asks Brenda in a weakly

voice. 'We didn't know where you were. Are you all right? May said she saw you going down the garden to the river. I'm sorry, I've been holding on for ages, Jess, but I've come over faint and I do need to go ... you know where. I can't hold on much longer.'

'I just popped out for some air, Brennie. Sorry you were worried.'

'You don't normally pop out for air,' she objects as I lever her up. Brenda is usually so sensible. Now she sits bolt upright, on the watch lest I escape, her eyebrows permanently raised, mouth slightly open. 'You could always open the window if you needed air,' she gasps.

'Don't you go opening that window,' says May in alarm. 'I'll catch my death of cold. I need to go too, Dee Dee. I need to go more than her.'

'Oh May, could you just hang on a minute? We shan't be long.'

'I can't hang on. I've been hanging on.'

Gently easing Brenda on to the toilet seat, I retreat outside the door, leaving it ajar. After several minutes, I ask if she is ready yet.

'No, not yet.'

'I can't hang on much longer,' announces May. 'I'll wet my knickers.'

'Brennie, will you be long?'

'I can't go,' wails Brenda.

'Perhaps you don't really want to go. Perhaps you only thought you did. What do you think, love?'

'I *do* want to go.'

Brenda weeps; May howls. Nathan arrives tottering to compound the emergency.

'May I offer you the use of the commode?' he chivalrously asks.

'Jess, I can't sit here any more. I'm too weak. I'm all

dizzy.' Brenda's stick-thin body begins to sag; her hands slip from the handrails. She is over-breathing.

'I don't think she's well,' I say to Nathan. 'I'd better get her to bed.'

'I've wet the chair!' May advertises. 'Dee Dee – will – you attend – I've wet the chair!'

Brenda allows me to drag her into the small spare bedroom we have downstairs and settle her in bed.

'I'm sorry, Jess, but I do need to go.'

'Well, okay, love, just go where you are. I've put in a pad so it'll be quite okay.'

'I couldn't *possibly*.' The grey, bunched face on the pillow looks scandalised.

'Love, it's perfectly okay. Nobody will know but me and I'll come in and sort you out in just a sec. May's causing (you know) a bit of a fuss. Could I just sort her out, darling, then I can come back and help you?'

The doorway is blocked by Nathan wheeling in my father's old commode, upon which he leans gasping for breath, having wrestled it out of the junk in the cupboard under the stairs. I swallow a scream. I summon all my patience and fortitude:

'Nathan, love, I don't honestly think that's going to help. You go back to the morning room, dear, and I'll just push the commode after you. You rest, you'll exhaust yourself.'

But Nathan, engaged in the Lord's work, is loth to budge.

'Let me be of service,' he begs, 'in any small way I can. Oh if *only*,' he laments, 'I were fitter and stronger.'

'If you were fitter and stronger, you silly old fart,' bawls May from the lounge, 'you wouldn't be here at all. It's all your fault, all this. If you hadn't wormed your way in, my Jacob would still be here. It's you that's driven him away. And now you won't let my son's wife be free to care for her mother-in-law's needs.'

Nathan mutters a selection of Beatitudes, laying emphasis on the blessedness of peacemakers, who shall be called the children of God.

Brenda moans aloud. 'Let her out,' she implores. 'Then she can look after May and come back to me.'

'It's true, Nathan, I can't get out,' I explain reasonably. Far down in the pit of my being a dark impatience stirs. A phantom hand rears and slaps, with satisfaction, a human obstacle. My own wrath scares me. He is only trying to help.

'The thing's jammed,' he acknowledges helplessly, striving to shake it by the handles. 'Oh dear.'

'You move away. There's a love. You move back a bit. Hold on to the rail, that's right.'

I shove at the dusty commode. Since it is well and truly jammed, I clamber over and wrench it back by the handles.

'Right, Mother, I'm coming.'

I clean May; change her clothes; scrub the seat and settle her comfortably again. I batter down the tirade of indignation that rises in my throat against her sham incontinence. She will neither meet my eyes nor in any way acknowledge me. It seems she holds me personally responsible for all her life's calamities: widowhood, old age, infirmity, and now the loss of her only son. Her jaw is set massive and firm against me.

'You all right now, dear?' I bundle the soiled clothes into sudsy water.

'No I'm not all right.'

'Then how can I help you feel all right, darling?'

She looks at me helplessly then, out of her fearful, watery eyes, pale as Jacob's.

'You can't,' she whispers. 'I don't think you can.'

'Well, I'll try,' I assure her. 'I'm trying my best.'

'Give me some pills, I want to die.'

'Don't be silly, May, of course you don't.'

'I do, I want to die,' she whimpers, and, rocking to and fro, croons, 'Do and die, do and die.'

'All's well.' I relinquish my efforts in this quarter for the time being. 'I'll be with you, May, when I've seen to Brenda.'

'I need to go,' insists Brenda, her face puffy with crying. 'I can't possibly go in a nappy, Jess. It's out of the question. Please just . . . let me try again.'

Her frail body perches on the toilet seat, knees together, thin legs apart like the wishbone of a chicken. My heart contracts at her vulnerable exposure.

'I can't go.'

'Perhaps it's nerves, Brennie. Try and take deep, deep breaths and remember everything's all right. Like this. All's – well. All's – well.'

'I think maybe I can go.'

'Oh *good*.'

'Well, I'm not sure. Do you mind going out and waiting?'

Several minutes pass, during which May is quiet, Brenda is quiet, Nathan in the morning room is nearly quiet, emitting only a holy murmur betokening his prayerful intercession on behalf of the household.

A tiny trickling implies God's answer to prayer.

'I've gone,' calls Brenda.

'Lovely, dear. Shall I come in and help?'

'No, because I still want to go.'

'Attention-seeking!' accuses May. 'Listen here, Brenda, we've only got one mother between us and I've as much right to her as you have. You've had your turn.'

I sway slightly, leaning against the doorpost, as I hear

my mother-in-law claiming me as her mother. Hot hate shakes me. The world carries on rocking.

I attempt a course of five deep breaths, counting backwards from ten to nought.

'I think you may have some kind of urinary infection, Brenda,' I confide in a steady voice. 'We'd better call out Dr Barnes just to check.'

'No, wait, no,' replies my aunt, who has a pathological nervousness of bothering the doctor. 'It's coming, it's coming . . .'

After a lengthy pause, the long-desired gush is accompanied by a great sigh of release.

Nathan ceases praying.

'Now I need to go again,' demands May. 'And be warned, I really mean it.'

By the time I have steered my mother-in-law to the toilet and back, an hour and ten minutes have passed since my return from the garden. I serve tea on the trolley in front of the television. The wraith of Jacob, driven out of the household during the fracas, steals back in to my weary mind; and I can see the dawn of that same awareness flickering in the eyes of the three old people he has left in my care.

And still he isn't back.

CHAPTER 3

They are still ringing, morning, afternoon and evening, Jacob's ladies, wanting his professional services.

'Oh is Mr Copplestone there? Only my tile's dislodged. So sorry to bother you.'

'Could you tell Jacob a bird's got into the cellar. Can he come and do something about it?'

Like a doctor he would do night calls if needed. Always he has that open-faced look that keeps him fresh and young; and a lovely manner, so trusting, so trustworthy.

I've been proud of him: *You're needed*, I used to say. *You're a needed person.* I encouraged him to answer the calls promptly; for I could imagine how helpless you must feel when you're a widow or even, God forbid, divorced, and suspect subsidence or cave-in in the fabric of your life. *He'll never let them down*, I boasted. *He'll never let anyone down.*

Now I have to tell them Jacob's not available at present, to see to their needs.

Not ill, I hope?

Er ... no, not ill.

Is he away? How long do you expect him to be, Mrs Copplestone? I really do need him. He fitted out my kitchen for me, you know.

We used to laugh over some of his ladies' pretexts for

calling him in, for it was natural that they should be a little in love with him, coming to regard him as a family friend rather than a joiner: looking surprised, and a touch put out, according to him, when he presented a bill. *She thought I double-glazed the whole house for love*, he'd say. *And hourly cups of tea. Honestly!*

Somehow we have got through five days of Jacob's absence, sleeping in snatches, the nights blighted by May's raving awakenings, at two, three and four in the morning, the time when one's private terrors trail the longest shadows. Clambering blearily out of bed, I nudge my toes into down-at-heel slippers and plod through to my husband's mother, keeping vigil with her as she ploughs her exhausting furrow through the night, gentling her panic as best I can.

Her rage with Nathan redoubles. As he shuffles out to clean his teeth in the morning, May shouts from her bedroom, 'Stop that marching up and down out there, you old fart! What do you think you are, the Salvation Army?'

'Bless you, May, you will have your little joke,' he whispers. 'But stay quiet now, there's a good girl, poor Jess has had a dreadful night. Up and down.'

'Little joke, my arse,' she grumbles, threshing and thrashing in her bed, grunting as if in combat with some demon, cursing the blameless person of the Reverend Rabbi Blue, whose 'Thought for the Day' she catches coming through the wall from Nathan's radio.

I go in to help May dress. Sometimes she fights the operation; the next day she hardly complains except to mention that she isn't a contortionist, is she, when requested to thread her arms into the cardigan.

I crouch and chafe May's hands, which are perpetually cold, with her poor circulation. She avoids looking into my red, tear-swollen eyes which affect her like a scald. I'm sure she has some notion that if Jacob has gone, so will I; or that I'll want to get rid of her now that her son, my husband, has gone. Through the fatigue and the sense of baffled dread, and a whole compound of emotions I am too tired and foggy to analyse, I try to reassure May that she won't be abandoned.

'We can help each other through, can't we, my love?' I coax, kissing the knotted vein on the back of her hand.

'Fat lot of good I am.'

'But you are, you are. Where would I be without you?'

'Free,' May replies, with defiant truthfulness.

'Oh, nonsense,' I brush her truth-telling aside, blankly recalling the tall woman loitering in the Square amongst the pigeons . . . was it only six days ago? She was free. I shudder.

'What would you like for breakfast, Mum?'

My apron is tied on and a resolute smile is stretched out on my face, held there by pure force of will.

May deliberates.

'Kippers,' she decides. 'I fancy kippers. Three kippers.'

'Oh sorry, May, I've none in. What instead?'

'Nothing then.'

'Well, I could offer you bacon, eggs, scrambled or boiled, sausages, toast, muesli.'

'If I wanted muesli I'd go to an Alp. I don't *want* muesli.'

'Muesli's ever-so good for you,' pipes up Brenda. 'And a lot easier for Jess to get when she's tired. I'll have muesli, Jess, and a piece of bread and apricot jam, if it's no trouble.'

Brenda, having recovered her self-control, is a little

parcel of bones set in rigidity of stress, a condition very bad for her joints, which are visibly more swollen since Jacob left. Setting a good dietary example, she glances hopefully at May.

'Oh, if getting my breakfast is too much trouble,' May erupts, 'then don't bother. No, Jess, don't bother. I'll have nothing. I'll starve.'

'It's no trouble, sweetheart.' I continue to hold the taut smile. 'You just say what you want and I'll get it for you.'

'No.'

I lip-read Nathan praying inwardly, *Please Lord make May ask for a bowl of cornflakes and eat it with a grateful heart.*

'Mum – ', I wheedle.

'Don't you *Mum* me, you're not my mum.'

'No, love. You're my mum.'

'I never am! Wash your mouth out, young woman! If you were my daughter, don't you think I'd recognise you? I had a *son* not a daughter, a son, and he's skid-addled.'

'Shush, dear, shush,' says Brenda.

'I won't be shushed. I'll have a boiled egg.'

May loves her food and cherishes contempt for people like Brenda and Nathan who eat sparingly. Having seen want in the 1930s, she still worries in case they reintro-duce the rationing of the '40s.

Mum. May is constantly calling me *mum.* Throwing the word with a kind of focused bale, as if playing quoits. Having been sagging from the waist, gripping a chair back to steady myself, throughout the discussion of who was mum and who wasn't, I recover and ask Nathan what he would like.

'Whatever is the least trouble to yourself, dear.'

I catch his covert, cataract-clouded eyes on my childbearer's body that has borne no children: wide hips, spongy bosom, maternal girth. These three are my sole brood, that will never fly the nest except into the next world. They will regress to helplessness, losing all command of function, all language, until reduced to the single word, Mother, repeated over and over again.

Nella. I think the name Nella. Nella flew.

'Let's all have eggs then, dears,' I propose briskly, opening the fridge door.

'As long as they're free range,' qualifies May who has been an Animal Liberation sympathiser since she became excited by the TV scenes of mayhem at Shoreham, the spectacle of genteel mothers and grandmothers sitting down in front of lorries, standing up to the burly law. 'We'll see you off, you meat-eating cannibals,' she says to Nathan, who doesn't reply. 'You'd eat your own mothers, you people, if they were served up in a tasty sauce. Mother-pie. That's what you carnivores go for.'

'You're on good form today, May dear,' he congratulates her.

'Oh am I, Ferdinand?'

And she rattles on about mad cow disease while Brenda with closed eyes sighs in her orthopaedic chair, gripped by the web of joint pains that flash and sing from knee to neck. Stoic and rationalist, Brenda masters her pain, and the mesh of terrors it fosters. I watch her now, mastering it for my sake; and it seems to me to be a noble thing, this control by mind over body. While carefully dipping her finger of toast into the cone of salt and then in the egg yolk, she reads out snatches of a letter from a fellow member of one of her pet societies, The British Hedgehog Preservation Society, whose headquarters are at Knowbury, near Ludlow.

This gentleman, a retired Colonel in his eighties,

voices passionate concern that the 'hedgehog horror' of last October should be averted in the coming autumn by a mass public awareness campaign. ' "People must be educated",' she reads in her thin, reedy voice, ' "to check in their bonfires of fallen leaves and other detritus for the presence of hedgehog-families which have made their homes there. Otherwise the Tamworth tragedy in which a whole family was burned by hooligans and at least one hoglet died, will be repeated again and again. How can we call Great Britain Great, or even civilised, where such wholesale tragedies are allowed to happen?" '

I half-listen to the talk of hoglets and leaflets as if from a remote distance, my gloved hands deep in suds, as quiet as Nathan who, up to now (again, I know, for my sake) has camouflaged his presence from May behind a wall of silence.

'I ponder in my heart what I can best do to aid you, Jessie, in the present emergency,' he told me last night. 'And I think I have the answer. I feel for you the most chaste, most grateful love. Do not mistake me,' he went on incomprehensibly, 'for one of those deluded antinomians who go round claiming that to the pure all things are pure. A doctrine I utterly deplore – fornicators and exploiters who use the Scripture to cover their own depraved lusts.'

'I never thought you were, dear,' I reassured him, tucking in the sheets.

On the bedside cabinet two heart pills, one red and one white, marked the point on the open Bible at which he would resume reading when he woke up next morning.

'A handy arrangement,' he observed. 'Because one turns automatically to the Scriptures, doesn't one, on waking – and it reminds one to take the pills.'

'Of course.'

I kissed him good night; he curled up and murmured that my arms were so chubby and strong. 'You are all that is womanly, Jessie,' he said. 'If I had married again after Bethan went to Jesus, it would have been a woman like Jessie Copplestone, someone pliant and caring, with arms shaped just like yours.' He paused, then murmured, 'And an ample bosom.'

All love has an underside.

But it is still love.

I understand, if not his theology, his loneliness; his inner chaos. How could I not understand it?

Jane Venner, the pastor's quietly spoken, strong-minded wife, has arrived to take care of the Oldies.

'Any news?'

'No.'

'Oh my lamb, let me give you a big hug.'

Hat off, gloves off, she announces that they will all do a nice jigsaw puzzle of The Houses of Parliament, which she has brought with her in her string bag. She upends the box, scattering a mass of pieces on to the table.

May, who is in awe of Jane, co-operates by sorting out river from building and sky as a dear old lady should, smiling feebly, muttering 'Judas' as she spots me putting on my raincoat. She's being abandoned. She looks terrified.

'Just off for a short walk and to do some shopping,' I explain, bending to kiss her cheek, which May averts. 'I shan't be long.'

'I've got to do this jigsaw,' May laments, stirring the fragments. 'One thousand bits. I hope you didn't get it at the Hospice Shop or the Heart Foundation, Jane, because there'll be half of it missing, and the whole thing will be a complete waste of time.'

'Don't worry, I can vouch for its being intact.'

By the time I am ready to go, Brenda has completed her allotted task of sorting the outside from the inside bits, and May has swept a modest gleaning of puzzle-pieces into her lap, there to stow them in the pocket of her cloud-grey skirt.

May steals her hand into her pocket, fondling the loot that allows her to demonstrate the imperfection of Jane's gift.

'One thousand pieces. Minus five?' she demands of Jane. 'What does that equal?'

'Nine hundred and ninety-five.'

'Just checking. They're selling jigsaws these days with *false solutions*. It's the Free Market Economy. Hardly credit it, would you?'

'Would you mind,' I hear Nathan ask Jane, 'if I retire briefly? I have one or two things to set in order?'

Brenda chats to Jane of hedgehogs; *such endearing creatures*, she is saying, *and they take care of garden pests – eat slugs, you know, for breakfast, lunch and supper*, and this zest is telling me to run along, to be easy in my mind about them, for all shall be well and all manner of things shall be well. She turns from my kiss to concentrate on the sabotaged puzzle. But May, fixing me with her eye, glowers on my treachery. I dither at the door, a conflict of emotion welling up so that I almost feel I can't go out and that it will be safer to huddle here, waiting for the phone to ring, and say he is dead, or he is alive.

That he is dead or he is alive.

'Oh yes, I'm very fond of hedgehogs,' agrees Jane.

'We fed one milk all last summer. . . . Go on now, Jess, and *don't* hurry, whatever you do.'

Out into the blaring don't-care trade and traffic I pass.

Jane tells me May has been ever-so good but that Nathan has been acting rather oddly, making numerous telephone calls with a lowered voice.

'Not that I've listened in,' she adds. 'But you can't help noticing when someone's being secretive, can you? He does look pasty and peaky. Honestly, Jess, how do you manage?'

'Hand to mouth.'

I am not far from tears: somehow I had made up my mind there would be a message, or Jacob himself, his tall figure with the slight stoop that only reinforces his height, standing at the centre of the room, saying apologetically, *I'm so sorry Jess, I was held up.*

'I went to church,' I tell Jane. 'It was quiet. And to the weir. He wasn't there.'

'Did you . . . think he would be?'

'Oh – not really. Just that he was, once. When Nella went. Our foster-child. He was devastated. But couldn't talk about it. Men can't, can they? He went missing. Only a matter of hours but I was worried sick. There he was on a bench at the Weir, Cathy had seen him, she came running in and said, "Your Jacob's at the Weir," so I cycled there and we sat together . . . and he said "You needn't have worried, I'd have come home." Eleanor's real mother wanted her back; we had to let her go. When I got there this time, I sat down where he'd been, and it's so odd, every man I see looks like him and seems to be calling something that sounds like my name. But they're nothing like.'

'I don't know what to say.'

'There's nothing you can say, is there? It's all right, don't worry, I'll cope. In the chapel there's such a scent . . . of cinnamon and blessedness.'

But strangely, God was not there in the chapel. I sat in its emptiness, my eyes roving the grave and solacing words which unscroll in simple golden lettering round the cornice of the Chapel:

PEACE, I read, PEACE

PEACE GRACE CHARITY FAITH HOPE LIGHT

No words are as beautiful. Yet they seemed so far away, too near to Heaven, unfurling there in the height of the tabernacle for all to see. I breathed in the quiet space of the sanctuary with its pale green walls, its arches and pillars of white and gold. I tried to pray but no prayers came. Here I was baptised by total immersion; here I first shared the communion meal as a girl of thirteen, sitting in the beech pew between my parents, with my own wafer, my personal beaker of wine; here I married Jacob; my parents were brought here in blond boxes, on the shoulders of our friends, Peter's and Catherine's fathers amongst the six. Dear souls echo here. But Jesus, Jacob, where were you?

Over the pews of the gallery slumped a mass of bedding, for the homeless, who are invited to sleep in the chapel through the winter season, have all been turned out now that it's spring and the weather is considered clement enough to allow them to sleep safely under the stars. There are thirty such people in Shrewsbury, at the latest count. My father would have been aghast at their intrusion into the chapel, the unshaven, the unsaved, snoring in his holy place.

I smelt the cinnamon before I left.

Is it cinnamon, or what, this scent? Spice, cloves of

some kind . . . ?

'In the chapel,' I told Jane, 'there's such a scent . . . of cinnamon and blessedness.'

Yes, but I didn't tell her that I prayed to Jesus, Jacob, and nobody answered.

At first I don't think there's anyone in Nathan's room. Only a stripe of light ribbons down the figure in the armchair. A shadow amongst shadows, he's reflected in the mirror which catches a glossy bead of light in one eye. He has his dressing gown on over his day clothes, giving the impression of a robe. Elbows resting on the arms of the chair, his narrow hands steeple at the fingertips, as if he were meditating an answer to a profoundly searching question put to him by the rabbinical figure in the mirror.

'Nathan,' I whisper. 'Am I intruding?'

'Of course not.'

'Are you sure?'

'Sure.'

'I just wondered where you were and thought you might be hungry. Time's getting on. I could bring you soup and a sandwich or something in here if you're happier – '

'I hadn't thought. Part the curtains, Jessie, would you – just a smidgeon. What time is it?'

'Nearly two.'

'So late?'

'Have you been asleep?'

'Goodness, no.'

He has been listening to a tape of the Brecon poet Henry Vaughan, he tells me, and roaming with him in the Holy Land. I cough and try to re-angle the conversation.

'Jane tells me you've been ... quite preoccupied today. Are you feeling all right, Nathan?'

'I'm not unwell, Jessie. I'm making ready.'

'For?'

'A short journey. A move.'

My eyes take in the bags on the bed; piles of neatly folded pyjamas and underwear.

'I've made an arrangement, Jessie (now don't be upset, my dear; just sit you down and listen, everything's quite all right) to enter a rest home.'

'Oh please – Nathan – no.'

'I'm afraid I made a silly, selfish mistake in coming here.'

'But how, love, how?'

'I tipped the scales. Before I came, you could cope, afterwards things fell apart. I'm not going to become less of a burden, Jessie. My mind gets scattered – I don't delude myself that it's likely to improve. I recall saying things to you last night that ... well, were – shall we say – foolish lapses. Without me, May will calm down, you'll see, and things will become more endurable and possible for you. It's the right thing, Jessie, I'm convinced it is.'

I sit very still, on the edge of his bed, beside all those carefully built and no doubt catalogued piles of clothes, my hands clasped in my lap. Nathan is a great one for making methodical notes on the backs of used envelopes. His whole life is here laid out and inventoried as if for kit-inspection on the bed. I itch to return it to the drawers from which it has been extracted. When I speak, my voice has a kind of desperate calm.

'Have I made you feel unwelcome, Nathan? Have I let you down in some way?'

He tells me no, never, I've made him feel the extent of human generosity and concern, no, that's not it at all.

'Then why are you leaving me?' I ask in the same frozen calm.

'To give you your life back. A little of it.'

'I don't want it back. I want Jacob to come back, I want you to stay here. I want everything to stay as it was. That's all I want.'

'I'll be very near if you want me, Jessie. Just round the corner. But not on top of you. I've made all the arrangements and Mrs Evans expects me in the taxi at 4.30. I'll of course ring and let you know when I've arrived.'

When I again remonstrate, Nathan fixes me with an eye that is at once compassionate and remorseless: he is acting on orders, it seems. Christ has spoken and, whatever his personal feelings may be, Nathan must comply.

'You have made me a most welcome guest here,' he says, gesturing to the room around him. 'But of course this has never really been my room. Inner space is where I live and have lived since Bethan passed on; I'm my own house, Jessie, crawling snail-like to God.'

May scoffs, 'He doesn't mean it, the old hypocrite. He's just attention-seeking.'

Nathan sits perched in his overcoat at the window, anxiously watching for the cab, knobbed stick in both hands.

'Thinks he's Jesus Christ making the supreme sacrifice,' May says, covering our silence. Her face carries a complex expression of truculent remorse. 'You'll be sorry, you potty old fool, when you've got yourself locked in there and can't get out again – you'll be laughing on the other side of your face then.'

'I'm not laughing.' His confidence has ebbed; exhaustion like a knock-down influenza shows in his quivering frame. 'Anyway, you won't have to endure me soon, May, will you? Be kind to Jessie when I've gone, May.'

'It's all those ninety-year-old women at the home will have to put up with you – that's who I feel sorry for – with a sex fiend in their very midst. Still, safety in numbers. *I'm* not a Sex Object,' she ended, 'whoever else may be – and harassment's a crime, I'd have you know.'

Surely, whatever this home may hold in store for Nathan, it will be less testing to his soul than May's parakeet feminism.

Brenda urges and I downright beg Nathan to reconsider.

'After all,' says Brenda. 'What do we know of this home? Remember The Brambles.'

'What brambles?' asks Nathan, preoccupied, craning, though it's twenty minutes until the taxi's due.

'Nathan, The Brambles Nursing Home. Don't you remember? In Baschurch.'

'Oh, I'm not going there. I'm going to Ivanhoe, dear, and we do know the matron.'

'It was closed down, Nathan, by the county tribunal,' I explain. 'It was an awful place. They didn't report the residents' falls or injuries to the Inspectors – and they denied them commodes and put buzzers out of reach. I mean, we don't know . . .'

'My dear Jessie, this matron is a Methodist!'

'But, darling, please, please postpone this – let me check it out more carefully, and see if there are better places, if you genuinely feel you must do this thing.'

Nathan reiterates with some dignity the fact that he has made all arrangements himself. Brenda concedes that if he is really sure, then we must respect his decision. May mutters that if The Brambles has been closed down, they should find a place called The Thorns or The Bed of Nails, since he thinks it's so damned holy to be spiked. This is her way of suggesting to Nathan the error of his ways.

His nervousness increases, sweating in the unnecessary greatcoat which he has decided to wear rather than pack, as a convenience measure. The taxi's four minutes overdue, four minutes and a half, if his watch is correct. Is his watch correct? We all compare timepieces, by which time the taxi is here. He licks his dry lips. His heart, which can't afford to pound, pounds.

'No, Jessie, I don't want you to come along. I can manage for myself. I'll be just round the corner, you know. So I won't say goodbye, just God bless.'

'Take care of him, Mr Parker,' I tell the driver. 'He's very, very precious.'

'Don't worry, Mrs Copplestone.'

'May I come tomorrow, and talk everything over?' I ask Nathan, diffidently, having stowed his frailty in the back of the cab, surrounded by bags. One does not know what Jesus may elect to forbid, now that he has taken over the detailed planning of Nathan's place of residence. My kiss flutters on Jacob's uncle's cheek. His fingers and mine briefly tangle, withdraw, and then touch again, a moth-like dither of indecisive gestures.

'Of course. You come along and visit me. And let me know at once – any news. Now there's a space, he may come home. And don't worry about my well-being. The matron's a lay-preacher.'

Now he is between worlds. Between haven and harbour. He and I are separately nowhere and terrified, myself drifting on prayerless swells, Nathan under full sail of prayer. As Mr Parker edges out, driving carefully with his precious cargo, I wave them out of sight, and the tears rain down. What did you mean, Nathan, 'Now there's a space . . .'? Were you holding on to the hem of some dotty bargain with God: Nathan for Jacob?

I am the space they have both left.

Chapter 4

'He was always forgiving me, that oily fish, he was always telling me I didn't mean any harm, it was sheer provocation,' May grumbles, in angry apology, in the stunned aftermath of Nathan's going, when I sit and stare concussed out of the window, and Brenda retreats to lie down for a couple of hours, having hugged me tenderly. I made sure not to lean too heavily, though longing for someone to lean on, sensible of her friable bones that are leeched of calcium by cortisone, and crack at the slightest knock, fracturing into new networks of pain, shrill and red.

'If I'd loved him more,' I confided to her in a whisper, 'I'd feel a less fierce remorse.'

'Look, he'll be all right. Think of yourself first. You're the needy one.'

May sees that too. She is threatened by that perception; offers me one of her heart pills.

'Come on, eat it like a sweetie. What you need,' she explains, 'is an aerial view.' She talks of the Dongas who live in tree-houses and prevent the devastation of the environment.

'No motorways up there, you see – no cars. No meals-on-wheels ladies do-gooding at your expense. Freedom. Now tell me, how long have you been a meals-on-wheels lady?' she enquires, as if conducting a poll.

'But I'm not.'

'Yes you are. If you're not a meals-on-wheels lady, who are you then?'

I put down the wooden spoon with which I'm stirring the tomato soup, and bring my face down to hers. Her gaze seems to blear and blur in genuine puzzlement. The face of the crouching woman is not one she exactly knows. She is viewing something senseless and unfamiliar. My face fails to add up. It is a twisted bunch of pain.

'Are you teasing me, May love?'

'No.'

'But you do know who I am. Who am I?'

'*I* don't know. If you don't know who you are, how do you expect me to know? Perhaps you need a counsellor. Everyone needs counsellors these days, so I'm told.'

'May darling, it's Jessie, your daughter-in-law.'

'Never heard of her.'

'Surely you recognise me.'

'Not really. Sorry. I recognise *her*,' she admits, pointing to her sister. 'But not you. Are you perhaps,' she suggests helpfully, '*secret*? You may be so secret you may not even know you're secret.'

'Jessie, she's having you on. She knows perfectly well who you are.'

'All I can say to help you,' May adds cordially, 'is that if *you* find out who you are and let us know, we'll write it down and learn it by heart – and anyone who comes to the door and wants to know, we'll show them the documentation if they query your identity. Until such time, we'll show them your temporary visa.'

'Right you are,' I agree. 'That sounds like a workable plan.'

Brenda explains that she would be all things to me, but failing powers prevent. In her need I took her in, but in my need she feels she can offer nothing more substantial than sips and pats. Not convinced that she shouldn't follow Nathan into the home, she mulls over this proposition as scientifically as possible, saying 'On the one hand' and 'On the other'. Her broaching this makes me feel quite faint.

'You'd be so much freer. And Nathan would have a familiar companion. You'd know we were well catered for.'

'Don't you dare. You're my right-hand woman.'

'But I can do so little.'

'There's such a thing as being... not necessarily doing. You're here with me. Don't even think of it. Promise; promise you won't.'

It's evening and she watches me wend down the tilting garden through a blue haze to the vague bank. I watch the shadowy swallows cruise in loops between the limes on the far bank and the rooftops on ours. They vault and dive, twitching to change direction, catching insects. A splash of blond light behind the trees is all that remains of the sun. My feet are drenched in these flimsy slippers.

We're both restless about Nathan. When we rang the home, Mrs Evans said he'd asked not to be disturbed; the move had taken it out of him. Behind her we could hear the jangle of crockery on a trolley, a muffled jabber of voices.

'Is it not possible,' I asked, 'for Mr Copplestone to have a room to himself?'

'Well, no, Mrs Copplestone. Your uncle has indicated

that his means could not stretch to a single room and in any case most of our residents do like to share. They enjoy the company and don't get lonely.'

My voice was tight: 'My uncle is such a . . . private man.'

'You'll find he's in with a very nice gentleman, quite a favourite with us all . . .'

'I *don't* want him to feel like a throwaway,' I said to Brenda when the matron had crisply closed the conversation.

The river spangles, pleating fast under Greyfriars Bridge. I park Brenda down on the river path in her wheelchair while I shop in Boots and the greengrocer's. When I return, two swans tack in our direction, stately and greedy: since we are human, we must belong to the bread-throwing breed.

'I've nothing at all for you,' I say, and after a brief wait they navigate towards a promising boy with a crisp bag, who tricks them by casting handfuls of dirt on the water.

Three helmeted cyclists hum past; ducks bob on boats' wakes.

Brenda says, dreamily, 'Perhaps it's something to do with Freud.'

'What is?'

'Well, I remember how May brought him up. I can see her now, slapping him around the legs for some minor misdemeanour. In her Strict Baptist days she always seemed to disapprove of him, though honestly, Jess, a better-natured lad could hardly have been imagined. He was a docile little chap who grew up into a quiet man, a family-man. He ought to have had three blond sons . . .'

A father in a tracksuit under the polled willow kneels to fasten one fair-haired child's shoelace.

'Three blond sons would have anchored him,' she muses.

I say nothing, unable to respond to such unconscious cruelty. The tension heightens in me, as if it were ratcheted up a notch; but I remain controlled.

'But you don't ... assume ... he's left us voluntarily, Brenda?' I ask, tight-lipped.

She cannot answer. I feel a deep anger stir; it focuses on the vulnerable back of her head, with its grey coil of thin hair through which the pale scalp shows in patches; an anger so profound that its merest swirl appals me into quelling it. Such an animus towards Brenda and all such aged burdens is an abdication that would make, if acknowledged, a lie of my whole life.

Something to say, I must find something to say that will anaesthetise us both.

'We used to drink from that fountain as children,' I remark, veering on to neutral territory from the dangerous area within. We pause beside the tree-high obelisk to John Clement, Surgeon and Mayor, in all its Victorian Gothic monstrosity. 'Let's see if it's working. No – it's all corroded.' I've stepped up to examine the rust-brown remains of the bowl with its sediment of last year's crumbled leaves. But when I turn back from the dried-up fountain, there is something not quite right.

It's all totally familiar, the disused house, its five windows boarded up, its compass of ancient trees, weed-lush garden; the curve of the broad path; the passers-by. Greyfriars has been the same since my girlhood. I've never thought about any of it. But now there's a sick estrangement in the stillness of blind stone. I catch my breath: the leaves agitate with unaccountable tremors and a rumour-monger's whisperings. Hints of some complicit understanding beneath the surface. Of me? Of it?

'What's the matter, Jessie?'

'I don't know. I don't feel right. I feel all over the place.'

Did that woman pass then, the stranger? While I clung to the handles of the wheelchair, dizzily, a woman I seemed to recognise passed with long strides, tall, with swinging dark hair, casting me a shy grin which froze when it wasn't returned. I couldn't place her until she'd gone.

We've brought chrysanthemums for Nathan, rust-red and orange.

'I don't know if flowers are allowed,' he whispers. 'Would you mind taking them home with you? Thank you for letting me see them.'

'But of course they're allowed.'

Nathan's singular spirit seems quenched. His eyes flit from face to face, scarcely resting. The cup rattles in his saucer with each failure to raise it to his mouth; the tea is cooled and on the point of becoming scummy. Brenda and I in floral armchairs sit with him in a triangular huddle in the middle of a roomful of residents: chatter-boxes some, silently vacant others. We glance round to appraise the standards of the place. All seems clean and wholesome; the residents are kempt, and kindly staff chirrup around and at them. This is quite a lovely room, with great picture windows yielding a glowing view on to cherry trees in early blossom and a magnificent hedge of red broom, high as a wall, whose wafts of scent as we came up the pathway replaced the residue of horror I was carrying in my breast with aching pangs of yearning.

'Have you been eating okay, Nathan love?' I ask, hanging on to the flowers.

56

'Oh yes. I had ... a sardine. It was delicious.' He appeases a passing nurse with a smile, to be rewarded with a friendly little pat on his shoulder.

'Only *one* sardine?'

'I only wanted one,' explains Nathan. 'I could have had three but I feared excess. So I stuck with the one. I was right, Jessie, don't you think?'

'Well, Nathan – darling – I do think you ought to eat properly. Eat as much as you want. It's not rationed, love, and sardines are very cheap fish. There's no question of greed.'

'Oh dear. You think I was wrong then?' His forehead furrows with bafflement and anxiety.

'Well – love – we worry for you. We'd so much rather you came home and be taken care of, where you belong. I never wanted you to come away,' I plead. 'It took me by surprise – and we never had a chance to talk it through.'

'But I'm here now,' says Nathan, grasping both chair arms as if apprehensive that someone will come and lever him out, displacing him all over again. His face is grey with exhaustion.

Brenda counsels, 'We mustn't put pressure on Nathan, Jessie. He's adjusting. It takes time.'

'That's right,' says Nathan. 'Just give me time, Jessie.'

'Of course, darling. I'm sorry.' The celluloid wrapping of the chrysanthemums rustles in my lap as I fidget. I'm almost crying with my need to collect Nathan back into the fold. His eyes at some moments so strongly echo Jacob's; their reminiscent blueness acts on my nervous system as poignantly as the scent of broom.

'It's just ... I wish *I had my back to the wall*,' he hunches forward. 'It's all the people staring, you know, Jessie. All so strange. And the space. It's like a ship's saloon. Makes me feel not quite right.'

57

'Well, I understand that feeling, all too well, Nathan. Let's ask the nurse if you can be moved, love.'

'Oh no,' he comes in quickly. 'You mustn't ask for special privileges in here, Jessie. Especially when you're a new boy. They don't like it. Much too busy.'

'Nathan, it isn't the army, love.'

'*Please* don't ask them,' he begs. 'Please.'

Where is Jesus, in this emergency? Has Jesus fled Nathan as he has vanished from me? Without Jesus, Nathan will be stranded. As the conversation develops, it is revealed that Mr Jones, with whom Nathan has to share a room, has involuntarily turfed Jesus out. John Jones is a jovial, life-and-soul-of-the-party sort, whose booming laugh drowns out the poetry of Nathan's life. He admires what he calls the nurses' 'chassis', and exclaims, 'Whoops, not amused!' when his quips meet the frost of Nathan's disapproval. Nathan pointed out to Mr Jones that he respected the nurses. Mr Jones replied that so did he respect them, the best lasses in the world. *They* didn't mind a bit of fun, he pointed out. Keeps life going. Cakes and ale, old chap, ha ha.

I see how awful this must be for our uncle; how such gusto would drown out the still small voice of God. I never felt so close to him as now. I never truly loved him until today. Before leaving, I hug him long and tenderly. He seems to focus on me fully for the first time.

'Any news, Jessie, yet?'

'Not just yet, dear.'

'There will be, you'll see. Don't you worry, Jess. It will all come right. Truly. Bless you both for coming. Love to May.'

My face hovering close to his, I instruct him, 'Eat. Or else.'

'Although . . . man shall not live by bread alone,' he reminds us, with a spark of his true spirit.

'But bread is God's gift too? Yes? Loaves and fishes? Nathan?'

'My Jessie.'

'I love you, Nathan. Will you remember that?'

From his country of exile, he watches our slow pilgrimage across what seem ten miles of carpet to the lounge door, where we turn and wave. He manages a bright smile and a fluttering wave.

'Toodle-oo,' he mouths.

'Oh, Mr Copplestone is such a nice, well-mannered man,' says matron as I enquire if he can be moved to a wall-seat. 'But you didn't mention he was incontinent?'

'He isn't.'

'Not to worry. I expect it's the stress. He should settle down before too long.'

'I'd like to pay the extra for him to have a room of his own,' I say. 'I'm sure he needs his privacy. He's pining.'

'Jessie . . .' Brenda pokes me with a bony elbow. I take no notice, though I have not looked into how things stand financially and it may be an impossible commitment. She audibly gasps when Mrs Evans names the sum involved.

'What option did I have?' I ask her afterwards.

'Oh,' says Brenda. 'Well. But it's a . . . *damned* . . . disgrace, pardon my French, the way the Council is closing these homes . . . four down . . . eight to be privatised . . . and all our lives we've paid our National Insurance and our taxes – all for this. It's so . . . *uncivic*, it is really. But, Jessie, you can hardly afford to promise away money like that. Can you?'

Fiona Claremont, our next-door neighbour, has been

sitting with May, winding wool into balls and then playing catch with the wound balls. Enthusiastic about the game, May requests Fiona to come again with further supplies of wool.

She asks us where we have been; have we seen her son?

'No,' I say, glancing down Fiona's list of callers. Catherine has rung twice, sounding urgent, says Fiona.

May is in full flow.

I feel I can hardly bear to be plunged so immediately into the turbulent tides of her mind.

'He was mentally defective, you know. It's true. We hushed it up at the time – and of course when a baby's asleep in its pram he looks quite normal. In those days there was a stigma attached. So we kept it hush-hush. He defected, you know. It turns out...' she leans forward, finger over lips, 'he was a *spy*.'

Theoretically, she acknowledges, with the Berlin Wall being down, it might be possible to go and collect him.

'Well?'

'Sorry, what, Mother?'

'Are you going to bring him home, or what? It's up to you. I can only advise on Foreign Affairs. It's your portfolio.'

Hers is environment, namely pollution, and she can tell us there's plenty of it about. Come back to Shrewsbury in ten years' time and there will be as much left of it as there is of Roman Viriconium, the way we're going on.

May's political extravaganza continues throughout supper, while Brenda and I sip soup, in a concussed silence ringing with uncommunicated questions. Since we fail to reply to her harangue, May invents foolish responses for us, quashing them with contempt.

'Anyway,' she swoops, 'where have you two been? Chapter and verse.'

When the word *Nathan* is spoken, she makes no direct comment but, looking round the room and loudly sniffing, says, yes, she thought there was an unpleasant odour in here: could she go to bed?

There is a look in her eye that notifies me of a grand-scale tantrum about to be staged.

I drag myself over to her and, balancing on the edge of her chair, offer an emollient cuddle. Cradling her head and brushing from her temples wisps of hair, I murmur weary nothings to her, to soothe her for the night. The rucked forehead smooths and she begins to relax.

'You're such an old crosspatch these days, Dee Dee,' she grumbles; but grumbles continently, as a matter of custom.

'Sweetheart, you'll have to overlook it if I'm sour from time to time – just understand, it's all the stress. Can you do that?'

May, satisfied with my climb down, agrees to wait an hour for bedtime, to allow me a chance to unwind before sorting her out. This concession is made with a majestic air of tolerance for the frankly feeble.

Anger again spasms. In coils of bowel deep-down rage seethes and curdles.

An indulgent smile twists my lips to comfort May: 'Better now, dear?'

I wish to God you'd shut up or go away.

Catherine, hooded against rain, is at the door, with a young man under an umbrella.

'Oh love, I've been trying and trying to get in touch. You remember Luke, don't you?'

The young man, tall and fair-haired, shakes out the umbrella, props it in the porch and follows us through to the lounge. A young man I only vaguely know is the last person I want to have to invite into my house and entertain.

'Jessie,' says Catherine, and she weeps. 'Please get ready for a shock. Luke has seen Jacob ... in Ludlow ... oh Jessie, he's alive, at least he's alive, love, which must give us hope.'

But she doesn't look hopeful. We stare at one another, and I don't cry but her tears pour down because she's gone through it all with me, and, Jessie, she says, Jessie, if she could take any of the pain on herself and carry it for me, she would. With her arms rocking my stiff body, she begs me please not to look like that. When she relinquishes me, I see with a kind of detached fascination that surplus breast-milk with which she is feeding Joe has bled through her T-shirt and slightly stained the breast of my blouse.

I need my inhaler; my breath grinds. Cathy rummages in my bag for it.

'Are you sure, Luke, can you be sure it was him?'

He draws invisible sketches on the carpet with the toe of one scuffed shoe, the pale-haired young man who comes in his shyness and his rue, with his sighting of the not-yet-dead. He flinches and winces all the way around his task, telling his story in a syncopated rhythm of hesitations and dashes. Catherine stands with me, adverse to Luke, side-to-side, arm round my waist, as if to testify that we are to confront this threat together. Her every gentle gesture tells me fiercely I am not alone.

Luke is sure. He wasn't at first. He was walking with his spaniel through Ludlow Market Square when he saw a man he thought he recognised waiting outside the butcher's: I would know the shop, he said, Reginald

Martin's, the chap who sells organic venison and venison sausages. Do I know the one? I tell him I don't know if I know it, it doesn't matter if I do, please go on.

'Anyway,' he continues on his faltering way, 'I saw this chap and thought, I know you, but I couldn't place him. He was looking at a string of wild rabbits hanging up by their feet outside the butcher's – gruesome sight, I always think, but then I'm a vegetarian – then I realised, and it gave me a real turn, it was Mr Copplestone – because Cathy... told me last week he was... missing. So I stepped up to him and said Hello Mr Copplestone, I don't suppose you remember me, I'm... something like that... and then this – person – came out of Martin's carrying a plastic bag, and said, Oh Jacob, would you... and he, well, he grabbed her hand, and they went rushing off through the crowd – and I took the liberty of following them, they went down Broad Street and off to the left, and I saw them go into a house in Netley Road – number 19. I've written the address down for you here, Mrs Copplestone.'

Alive.

A person with him, said 'Oh Jacob'. A she.

You are alive.

My Jacob.

Not mine.

She said Oh Jacob, he snatched her arm and scrambled her off. The scrap of paper says 19 Netley Road, Ludlow.

'Oh Cathy, he's alive,' I say tonelessly.

A line of rabbits is strung along the window-ledge. Yes, I do know the butcher. Their soft eyes are blindly open, their pelts grey and white. The manner of their death is hidden from the customer, their wiped wounds being turned inwards to the wall. I cannot react. I see the rabbits quite clearly. The silence is broken only by Cathy's sobbing. I remind her of the baby.

'Joe will just have to cry and be hungry. It won't kill him. You come first at the moment. Of course you do.'

I look at her with a certain wonder. When, at some future time, I come to reflect upon this, I shall be moved that Cathy put me first for, after all, we're ... only ... friends, not – kin.

'Not kin,' I say.

'Pardon?'

'Did she have ash-blonde hair, the – person?'

Luke did notice that she was very fair.

'Ah,' I say quietly. 'I think I know the one; I've glimpsed her. You should go home now, both of you – and thank you. I need to ...'

'But will you be okay on your own?' asks Catherine.

That question carries a huge echo.

Gull-high I hang above Ludlow Hill, sweep with aerial view along well-known streets, cobbled alleys where faces bubble and dissolve, but no one I know.

'Yes, I'll be fine.'

'But can I stay the night, Jessie? I've told Alan I might. I can just go home and pick up Joe; we can keep you company. I mean, you wouldn't have to have me in the room with you, but I'd be there if you ...'

The strangest night I've ever had. No Jacob in the big bed but Cathy and Joe lying beside me. And sometimes my face is lying against her breast and we are whispering ... odd ... recalls of childhood incidents, fishing for tadpoles in the mere, climbing trees ... dreamy picturings of my adored Nella in a boat ... driftings to half-sleep, waking with the certainty that Jacob has died, I've seen his grave ... crying out then, as I remember, and Cathy who weeps so easily wakes and joins in . . . the lulling warmth of her body against mine, ample like mine, her breasts so hard with milk . . . Joe's nappy-smell, his greedy mouth leeching milk . . . he never cried once all night but then he had no reason to cry, Cathy being there on tap . . . and once I bent over her as she slept and kissed her temple, and she did not stir. I saw the dawn in and it was so strange to think that you, Jacob, were going through the self-same night in Ludlow, lying in another bed with another woman, with whom you must have planned to vanish – without telling me . . . and this enormity could not be conceived by my brain, it seemed to swell like some monster you'd fathered on me . . . and I reared up in bed, holding my bursting head, on Jacob's side of the bed, but Cathy woke and knelt up, holding me fast in both her arms and rocking me, putting me first.

The eyes of the baby were wide open when we looked at him, and entirely peaceful.

Chapter 5

'Did Jacob love me, Brennie? Did you think – I mean, did you doubt – he loved me?'

'Of course he loved you, Jessie, of course he did.'

She lists the evidence as she sees it.

He'd always kiss me goodbye when he went off to work: without fail. He did all the things husbands do for wives.

He laid the patio for me and lugged the stones through for the rock garden. He might have been a bit lax about maintaining the house but that was because he was so busy with other people's.

He never complained about his food being late when May had been causing mayhem.

He drank little, though he secretly smoked.

He was a good husband and a kind nephew.

It sounds a modest-enough obituary for someone I have all-but worshipped.

I query the smoking. 'I don't think he's ever smoked, Brennie. He hated cigarettes. He always said it made people's mouths smell.'

Perhaps she was mistaken about that, Brenda unsteadily admits.

'But – Brenda – *why*? why would he – just ... go away and vanish?'

She agrees that these actions cannot be squared with the Jacob we knew.

'Do you think,' she moots, 'that it could be one of these funny turns men have in middle age, that you read about?'

'Menopausal?'

'So he might . . . grow out of it?'

'I don't know.' We gape at one another from a suddenly revealed chronic ignorance.

'I had a manfriend once,' she confides. 'So I have a faint idea of how their minds work. Yes – a fellow geographer. We were, you know, on similar wavelengths, at least as regards the Shropshire Wildlife Trust, of which we were both life members.'

I am momentarily diverted: Brenda so rarely makes personal revelations that one assumes she has none to make.

'So what happened, Brennie?'

'He went off and married a historian, a very nice woman. Chubby.'

'Poor Brennie.'

'Not really. I've had a good life. I only mention this to show that I have had some small experience of how a man can just . . . discard a person. Very odd. Of course I had seen some signs. A cooling of relations generally. I believe they lived very happily at Market Drayton. A place I do not much care for.'

'What are you going to do?' she asks me.

'I don't know.'

I hunch at the morning-room table with a mug of tea. Cathy has long been gone, taking with her most of the strange, transfigured anguish of our night together. I feel inert. My mind sluggishly pursues questions it would rather evade. Were there signs I missed? There must have been. There must have been a whirlwind of hectic secret activity on the other side of a soundproof screen as I went about my day-to-day obligations, bathing his mother, cleaning his house, getting him to pass me his glasses so that I could clean them. I am for the moment rather numb than hurt at these thoughts.

But the house is dirty; it's a mess.

I begin to clean. Brenda objects: 'It doesn't need cleaning, Jessie stop it,' but I tell her it's a mess, an impossible mess, we can't go on living in such a mess.

'Jessie, stop it at once.'

'But it's chaos.'

I am finally persuaded to relinquish my cloth.

Brenda, doing her best to keep her head, searches in herself for ways to perceive this anarchy as a peculiar sort of variation on the norm.

She ventures to suggest that it's the kind of thing they report in *The News of the World*, or that if you were a *Cosmopolitan* reader you would instantly recognise.

She's sure there must be a statistic.

Statistics are comforting. They imply that you can get a grasp of delinquent facts by measuring them on a graph as trends and tendencies. Jacob's behaviour is almost certainly part of a larger problem caused by Modern Life. 'Trends and tendencies,' she keeps saying.

But maybe it's a blip.

If it's a blip, Jacob will come home, tail between his legs. Jacob will resume being Jacob, supposing it's a blip.

I find myself looking at her quite coldly, blackly.

I've said for twenty years: what matters to me is you. I want your good, all of you, I want to listen to you, care for you, and I don't ask anything in return.

Blessings poured into my lap for twenty years.

I've needed to bind them together and to me, so that

we connect at many points, a mesh of belonging, and in turn the web of my design links with other women's weavings of people together so that ultimately all bond; all may be one.

But Jacob has said: I'll not be bound. He's broken the delicate threads woven from my own insides that hold us in loving fellowship; and everyone has said, we accept your services but never mind the theory.

'Are you all right, Jessie?' asks Brenda, looking frailer than ever.

'Fine. How about you?'

I find myself drumming on the table with my finger-tips. It must be quite annoying for Brenda but she doesn't complain.

Jacob has as good as told me: you are not my next-of-kin.

So how come he has left me with all his relatives to care for?

Brenda is silent, over-breathing. She confesses, 'I think I need to go to the loo and I'm not sure if I can get there – it's all been such a shock. I'll try.'

I support her, without offering the kind words she needs and is entitled to expect, to steady her, for suddenly I can't trust myself to speak, afraid of what uncaring words will spill out. But the part of me that is still the Jessie I need to be is fearful of the damage that will be caused to the dear person of Brenda by the venom that is in me. I stand, gracelessly dumb, outside the door and wait. The vicious part is thinking, *Jacob should be doing this, not me*.

Jacob is in Ludlow having orgasms. He hasn't time to spend waiting outside the lavatory door for hours on end.

Jesus washing the disciples' feet was always my pattern. I've spent so long grovelling around down here looking for feet to wash. Everyone's done their best to oblige.

All the children I never had come rushing down the pavement outside my window on skateboards.

A mind-storm.

Three times Brenda and I make the round trip between lavatory and sitting room, during which excursions I offer scarcely a syllable of encouragement – although I know perfectly well that part of her bladder-problem is emotional, and that I could more rapidly solve the problem through showing compassion. Still I elect to withhold that compassion, the more to let my sores fester. Drearily we march together to and fro.

She sits on the pan and weeps, 'I'm a burden.'

The house is evil with my silence.

'Mum!' shrieks May from her room.

I do not respond.

'Mum! I want you!'

'May – I am not your mum,' I advise her in a tensely level voice. 'Will you please stop calling me Mum.'

She's not my mum either, come to that. She's Jacob's.

'Have it your own way,' she shrugs. 'I suppose you are a member of Mothers' Liberation. Well, it's high time they had a Front. Now would you just help me pull this stocking up, Hoojamaflip . . . thank you kindly.'

I haul up the tights as she wriggles into them. I feel no movement of tenderness as arm-in-arm we navigate into the morning room.

'I could just fancy scrambled egg and bacon,' announces May eagerly. 'Lightly scrambled, mind, Jess, don't over-cook them or they go all dry. And fried bread and maybe some fried tomato.'

'Oh May, don't bother her, dear, she's too tired to go cooking for your breakfast,' says Brenda, trying to control her deep agitation and to impress May with the importance of not putting pressure on me.

'It's okay,' I say tonelessly, bending to fetch the frying pan from the cupboard, scooping margarine and melting it. These simple and mechanical jobs are somehow a grinding effort: the pan a heavy weight I lug up, to crashland it on the cooker so that everyone winces. Tears are building behind my eyes, but not tears of grief: tears of rage and frustration at being trapped in this kitchen, slave to these old women, hating myself for resenting them – while Jacob . . .

Jacob.

I place the dish of egg and bacon down in front of May with exaggerated care; for a phantom Jess is slamming the plate down and shouting words of bale. Brenda chews her toast and marmalade quietly.

I sit at the window with my cup of tea, eyes fixed on the river, the wall of tears building and building; whenever I raise the cup to my lips I have to return it to my saucer untasted.

'What's up with her?' murmurs May to Brenda between mouthfuls. I can't look at her.

'She's upset – too much for her.'

'You wait till I see that boy,' says May, munching. 'I'll leather him – I'll lather him – I'll tan his hide – he won't sit down for a week.'

'Shush, May, do.'

'I won't shush. Why should I shush in my own house? I won't have that lad upsetting my mum and that's the end of it.'

As I wash up she explains the benefits of alternative medicine; and how there is not only the delightful Chinese lady at the AcuMedic Centre on Wyle Cop who will stick me full of pins but a gentleman aromatherapist advertising in the *Shropshire Star*. This paragon lives out at Nobold but will do home visits, so that I be spared the trouble of stepping out of our front door to obtain the benefits of evening primrose, juniper and rosemary massages. May will pay for these out of her Attendance Allowance; it's the least she can do for a good mum such as I've been to her.

When the phone rings, May takes the call.

'Who's that? – it's him, Jessie, it's him. No, let me speak to him, I want to speak to him,' she clamours, as my sudsy hands reach for the phone. She cradles it to her ear. 'After all, he's my – so-and-so. Now then, you, what have you got to say for yourself? ... Oh, you do, do you? Well, my laddo, you're not going to be allowed to speak to her until you've explained yourself to me ... Are you doing drugs, or what? ... Well, I suggest you pack your bags this minute, and come back home where you belong or I shall personally make it my business to come over there and detoxify you.'

The phone is in my hand.

My husband says, 'Hello, Jessie, Jacob here.'

'Jacob.'

His beautiful, tender, reliable voice.

'Jessie,' says that familiar voice, 'I'm *so sorry*. Can you ever forgive me?'

'Oh ... love. Are you all right?'

'Yes, I'm all right. Are you all right?'

'I thought you were dead.'

'I'm sorry.'

'Jacob, I thought you were dead.'

'But I'm not.' He sounds embarrassed.

'Are you coming back?' I ask in my waif-voice, my wraith-voice; and immediately wish I hadn't asked, in case the answer is never.

'I ... don't think so. I don't think I can. I'm sorry.'

'Oh.'

'Jessie?'

'Yes.'

'Are you still there, Jessie?'

'I'm still here. Are you still there, Jacob?'

'I'm still here.'

I panic. 'You won't just ring off, will you, and leave me in the dark – and leave you nowhere – where I don't know . . . how to contact you?'

He sucks in his breath. Is mastering his guilty wish to bolt from this uncovering of my distraught pain: I can hear that wish.

'No. It's all right. I've got loads of pound coins.'

'You're in a phone box?'

'Yes.'

I imagine Jacob in a phone box; see him blurred through smeary glass, tall frame stooping, a pile of pound coins beside his elbow.

'Give me that phone back,' demands May. I'm off-guard and she is able to grab it. 'Now see here, you – on your bike, back home *at once*, I'm not having you staying out till all hours, you're underage, I'm not having it and neither is Dee Dee and neither is Brenda and neither is – '

Frenzy grips me. Tearing it out of her hands, I thrust her back into her chair, where she sobs out, astounded, that she was only trying to help. I pay no attention. He may ring off and I'll have lost him again.

He's still there.

'It's May, she's . . . rather agitated,' I explain.

'Jessie, I'm sorry to have landed you with all . . . our responsibilities. But I didn't see any way out.'

'Oh, Jacob.' I am weak at the knees, I am buckling, my insides swoop as they turned over and over in faintness as a young girl in my first passionate love of him; as when Nella came to be our child and was taken away; as when we thought (mistakenly) I had conceived, but it was only an early menopause. 'Oh Jacob, it's so beautiful to hear your voice again.'

He coughs, rushes his words. 'Good to hear you, Jess. I'm just really sorry . . . the circumstances . . . you don't deserve this . . .'

I recover myself. 'Don't say sorry again, love. It's not necessary. Truly. Could you just . . . try to explain what's happened . . . so that I'll understand . . . Please, May, shush. *Please.* For the love of God – shut – up.'

May is roaring something incomprehensible; drumming with her feet; the side-table collapses at a blow from her flailing arms and a half-drunk cup of tea is pitched flying.

Brenda, losing all patience, smacks her hand: 'Stop it.' Brenda's arthritic hand flinches with the pain; May, quite unhurt, is only stimulated by the blow.

'Brenda hit me! Brenda hit me!'

'I can't hear you, May's having a tantrum.'

'I'm not so.'

Jacob says, 'Put the phone down, Jess. Then unplug it. Go upstairs and I'll ring you on the extension.'

Bounding up the stairs, leaving May's foghorning to die into a spurned silence, I am unsure whether he will ring back.

The phone rings: Jane Venner.

'Go *away*, Jane, I'm expecting an urgent call.'

Manners out of the window. My life hangs panting on the need to hear him again.

'Jessie, did you go upstairs?'

'Yes. It's private here. I am wondering . . . if you can explain what's happened, and maybe we can sort it out together.'

'Can I just say first, Jessie, that there's a cheque in

the post. I closed the Building Society Account. I hope you didn't mind. Your half is on its way.'

'Yes, never mind about that. Are you ... with someone, Jacob?'

'Do you mean this minute?'

'No, I mean, living with ... in love with?'

He admits, in a small voice, 'Yes. Sorry, Jessie. It was the last thing I wanted.'

'Are you living in ... Catherine's cousin Luke said he saw you in ... Ludlow?'

'Yes, I saw him. He's been to the house today and said ... he and Cathy told you. I feel such a shit – sorry but it's the only word. I'm not living here for good ... just staying for the time being, doing the occasional odd job till it's sorted out where to live in Shrewsbury.'

'Oh. Right. And you think it's serious? You don't feel, at present, that you'll decide to come back?'

'Hang on a sec. I'll just put in another coin. Don't want to get cut off. I'm not coming back, Jessie love.'

He called me Jessie love but said he was never coming back.

I pack this wound with swathes of lint. It smarts raw and new beneath the wadding of gauze. I distance my mind from this smarting. It is important to keep calmly talking, gleaning, smoothing, soothing Jacob into surrendering up his secrets.

'Could you say why, love?'

There is a pause. I hear Jacob take a breath to speak but no words come out.

'Take your time. It can't be easy to explain. I promise I'll try to understand,' I woo him.

'Well, it's ...'

He's never been good with words. He'd leave those to me. Sometimes I'd even answer for him: it could be quite comical. He'd say, *What do I think about that, Jess?* He'd ask me if he liked such-and-such to eat.

'Just anything you could say that would help me understand.'

'I met a woman, you see . . .'

'Uh huh?'

'And – I did try, Jess, I honestly tried not to . . . but I couldn't stop thinking about her. And she'd been just divorced, left with two small children, and I felt for her. She's had a hell of a life. Her husband knocked her about. So I was . . . drawn to her. It doesn't mean I stopped feeling . . . affection . . . for you. It's hard to describe. But it became so that I couldn't bear to be away from her. And I felt I couldn't tell you.'

I swallow, then swallow again; the dry lump in my throat can't be swallowed. It is made known to me that the person 'is a blonde', she is in her late twenties; has done a course in Hospitality Skills at a college of Further Education. A mirthless laugh rises in me and dies. Jacob sees nothing funny. He goes on to explain that she doesn't work of course because of the children being so little.

'How old are the children, Jacob?'

'Three and five.'

'So really you're a sort of . . . family?'

'Er – well, they are. Oh Jessie, how awful this is for you.'

'Could you tell me, Jacob, was it in any way my fault? Was there anything I was doing or should have done and didn't, that if I'd known could have prevented this happening? – I mean, one can be . . . so blind, just getting on with life, being busy and so forth. Is there anything I could have done?'

'Good God, no. Except perhaps, don't take it wrong,

you were . . . too good for me. I always felt that. The way you took the Old Ones in . . .'

'I thought *we* did. We took them in.'

'Well . . . it was more you.'

'But it was *for* you! Jacob, it was because they are *your* people. You see, it's been such a shock, I'd felt we were happy, we had a good marriage . . . and it turns out I was mistaken, and I never suspected . . . I never imagined . . . I was getting it wrong all the time.'

This has burst molten from my numbness. I stop short, because there is more of it, far more, and far more emotional, which I must not be.

'Jessie – I've known you almost all our lives – I've known you as such a good person – I thought you must somehow feel it was your job – your Christian duty, your duty as a woman, if you like – to have the Oldies in your care. I suppose I thought of you as somehow – a carer – just as I'm a joiner.'

'Yes, I see.'

'Do you?'

'I think so. I think I'm beginning to.'

'I hate to hurt you.'

'Thank you. Don't put the phone down, Jacob, will you, I'm not ready to put the phone down, I'm not steady yet.'

'No, of course I won't. Of course. Don't worry.' He reassures me as he used to do with his ladies, in that dependable voice which I can still not persuade myself to believe is only air. 'If the coins run out, I'll go and change a fiver at the newsagent's, don't worry.'

'Okay. Thanks.'

'And of course, it was never really . . . right, sexually, between us, was it?'

'Wasn't it?' I ask faintly, faintingly.

'Well . . . oh dear, I seem to be putting my big foot in

it, I don't seem to be able to say the right thing, I'm sorry. I feel awful about what I'm doing to you, Jess.'

Is he pleading for absolution? So soon? Before I've even understood the nature and extent of my injury? There is something so – not quite casual – but shallow – in his remorseful words that a quick contempt stirs. He wants me to make it better, that's the feeling I get.

I say nothing.

'How are the Oldies?' he asks.

'Nathan admitted himself to Ivanhoe,' I say in a flat voice. 'He felt he was a burden. May is ... much as usual – Brenda is a bit shattered. What shall I tell them from you?'

'I don't know.' His voice is hazy, his eyes must be glazed as he ponders the old family he's disowned in favour of the young family he's espoused. Jacob sounds suitably wretched as he tentatively sounds me out, saying, 'What do you think, dear?'

The endearment tricks me into colluding, conspiring, a couple determining a joint plan of action: though part of me detects the trick with forensic accuracy and is not deceived.

'The truth, I suppose,' I suggest.

'Yes, probably. Can I leave that to you?'

'Right. Right.'

'You'll get the cheque first post tomorrow. Money's a bit tight this end, Jessie, we'll have to sort things out properly in due course, you'll have enough to tide you over. Hazel has trouble getting maintenance out of her ex. He was a right swine. But I won't leave you in want.'

'Thank you,' I murmur. It wasn't meant as sarcasm; money concerns seem so unreal that I can't respond appropriately. And the name, Hazel, sticks at a painful angle in the sensitive tissue of my mind. A named person is so much more real and potent. Hazel is blonde. Hazel has two children.

'Don't be bitter,' he urges.

'I wasn't,' I say in surprise. 'I've not really taken it in yet, Jacob. I'm shocked ... I'll need to absorb it all.'

'You're such a strong woman, Jessie,' he reminds me, and evidently reassures himself by maintaining this fact. It makes me sound grotesquely like a prizefighter or weightlifter. I'm being primed to carry them all on my colossal shoulders wherever they need to go. He says it's a relief to him to think what a coping person I am.

'I don't feel very strong,' I reply, without pressing the point.

He will phone again later in the week.

He won't let me down.

He promises.

He hopes I'm not too unhappy.

Please would I not try to contact him; things are a bit tricky. He will definitely be in touch, I can rely on him.

He's sorry he can't do much to help.

He still cares about me, he wants me to know that.

He'd better be off now, there's a queue outside the box.

Okay, Jessie? Is it okay for him to ring off now?

He goes.

He's left me with phrases that pierce and penetrate me through and through. A blonde: a woman who's a blonde. Not fair-haired, not blonde, but a blonde. Jacob could talk about a woman like that, picking her up by her hair.

Which does not make me a brunette, dark though my hair is, and greasy now, I see in the wardrobe mirror, flecked with a scatter of coarse grey hairs.

Such a woman cannot compete with a blonde.

I hadn't known I was in a competition. Had thought that I was just accepted and loved as myself; the person I am, uniquely Jessie. The sharp novelty of rejection comes as a flash of revelation. So this is how it feels; how they feel, the many people I've pitied for being ditched. There are so many ways to ditch us: in the street or boxed up in a house. At least I've a shelter over my head.

He'll not come back. He's got two children now.

Didn't say whether boys or girls, or one of each. How he grieved when Nella went comes back sharply; keening in one of the third floor rooms. Standing outside the door with bent head, I listened to him weep. And when he came out, dusk had fallen; his eyes were swollen. We walked downstairs hand in hand but did not speak. A barren couple.

But he said ... he said ... it had been no good sexually between us ... he said that.

He said it was me that took the Oldies in. Not him.

He said his blonde had had a hell of a life, and therefore he had pitied her.

Did he take that sweater?

I really ought to chuck it out, he'd say, reluctantly, season by season. *It's awful.*

Don't you dare, I said. *That sweater's you. You wouldn't be you without that sweater.*

I rummage for it now, to crush it up and bury my face in its dark brown wool. It always held the scent of Jacob; I could breathe it in to recover him when he was away. I'd rarely wash this sweater, which now I locate and pull out of the drawer. It's his masculinity I smell here, the tenderness of his maleness in the fibres ... I never put it to myself like that before ... but twenty years of his wearing it had shaped it comfortably to his darling body. I'd darn the holes and sew in frayed edges;

never put it away without pushing my face into the fabric, knowing him there.

I lie now with my face drowned in its friendly darkness. His scent is still here: musky, spicy, though a little faded and staled. Salt of his sweat is joined by salt of my firstborn tears, only a few; I daren't give way.

I never sought my own pleasure. My bliss rode on the back of yours. And when you groaned and fell limp, sighed, rolled off drowsy and tender, that was such shining for me. I told myself I could give you everything you needed in this world.

But you say it was no good.

It was union.

No good? How can you say that, how can you say that? I've always been shy to say the word sex. Sex wasn't what we had. How could you call sex this presence of Christ in us? I'd felt our souls met. The Song of Solomon not a *Marie Claire* article.

I didn't always deeply enjoy the act, it seemed so quick and crude. But I offered myself through it to you. And I enjoyed your pleasure.

This garment has an almost sourish tang, like stale cigarette smoke. It is pleasant and also unpleasant.

I blank out and when I come to, muzzy from my shallow doze, the fog of some detestable thought lingers in me without exact shape, but to the effect that the world is nothing like the dream I'd cooked up: but offal, sauced.

No, I spit out the cold remains of that thought.

I call to you – come back to me – you belong here – you do – come home – Jacob – do. If lightwaves can travel home to our eyes across boundless space, can't souls?

The air is so dead in here, the window's been painted

in. I kept mentioning it to him but something else always cropped up.

For comfort I pull on the sweater, dragging it down over my breasts, tummy and hips. A brown bolster of a woman bulges in the sweater of a slender man. Dumpy lady with shortish dark hair that needs washing; puffed eyes which used to be congratulated as nice eyes, sweet eyes, full of lovingkindness; but not now. Puzzled and bovine. Can this suety body be the temple of the Holy Spirit?

I struggle out of the sweater, which I bundle into the laundry basket. When it is washed, it can go to Oxfam. It would be a shame to waste it.

CHAPTER 6

How could it possibly be my fault? Brenda asks me.

'I must have driven him to it.'

'That is plain daft. How can you be so ridiculous?'

'But what other reason can there be?'

She can't hazard a reply to this question until she has thought it through, and her scrupulous pause creates a space into which my unreason can pour. Somehow I recognise it as unreason even while I hold it forth as possibility; for if the fault can be attributed to me, I may assert control over its remedy.

'You see, there just isn't any other explanation. I've neglected him – I've made him feel unloved. Perhaps if I go and beg him to forgive me, he'll come back, Brennie, he'll let us try again? I'll be able to put him at the centre of my life for a change . . .'

I twist the sodden handkerchief between my hands; am never still. I've become a ghost of my ample and competent self, to whom they all referred for the knowledge that the world was, in the end, a good place to be. No longer mobile and active, I've dwindled to the compass of the armchair Jacob vacated, from which I drag myself to perform the services required.

'I could slim. I could dye my hair.'

'Don't think things like that. They are so . . . utterly beneath you.'

'So I've always thought . . . but look what's happened as a result,' I burst out in anguish. 'I've lost him to a *blonde*.'

'For heaven's sake. Who cares what colour her hair is?'

'He does.'

'Then he's a fool.'

'He's Jacob. It never crossed my mind he bothered about things like that . . . perhaps all men do, do they, Brennie? . . . I feel I understand so little any more . . . all I know is, I got something so wrong. All that time. All those years.'

'Higgamus hoggamus,' she blurts.

'Pardon?'

'The social anthropologist . . . forget the chap's name now, who woke up one morning with this rhyme going in his mind . . . which he said was the solution to the incompatibility of the sexes:

> Higgamus hoggamus
> Woman's monogamous.
> Hoggamus higgamus
> Man is polygamous.'

'But is that true, Brennie? Can you honestly believe it all comes down to that?' I stare at her, baffled.

'I don't know. There may be something in it, mightn't there?' she ventures.

'No, I don't think so. No. I won't believe that. Think of all the faithful couples we know.'

She doesn't ask how we know they're faithful.

May is charitable about my violent behaviour as I tussled for the phone. She refrains from alluding to how I muscled into her conversation with her son and thrust her back into her seat, except through certain significant nods in my direction and a tendency to edge around me as a beast of unsound temper. She is saying, in her own way, *Not so perfect, are we, any more*; an insight I dumbly acknowledge.

Behind her performance I recognise the dread of abandonment she is denying. It is the same as my own. I can only fall back, with Brenda's social anthropologist, on the jingling rhythms of 'higgamus hoggamus'; my mind travelling the well-remembered streets of Ludlow, walking by the Teme from Ludford to Dinham Bridge, through forests of beech and hornbeam. With Jacob and Nella, in another world. The chalky rock by the riverside powdered your fingers like talcum, and in the moist fissures mosses and ferns greened the cliff. His being in Ludlow with this blonde woman shocks me like a trespass, a blasphemy. It was so much our place. In autumn the hips and haws up at Whitclyffe grow big as baby tomatoes, and the path, over-arched with beech, creaks softly underfoot with fallings of mast, sycamore seeds, acorns, oak leaves. And it is here that Jacob has chosen to betray me. I remember a flight of rock steps, with a notice reading, 'Danger. Sheer Drop.'

My ghost wanders there, up and down, up and down, till I am sick of the blighted memory of the place.

When May sensibly points out that life must go on, I shudder. The mere thought of having to get through all the minutes that compose today enervates me. She suggests a nice walk to the Dingle.

'A nice walk,' she insists thirty-four times. She enquires am I deaf, because if so the nurse will syringe my ears?

'A – nice – walk – to – the – Dingle,' she repeats, and keeps it up, in a monotonous rhythm, fist hammering the arm of her chair.

In the end, I capitulate, in a kind of stupor of concession: 'Why not? If that's what you want, May.'

He'll not ring again today. He's done what he takes to be his duty.

Peter will come and push Brenda's wheelchair; I'll push May's, and Catherine and the children will meet us there. As I am lurching about gathering our belongings together, Deborah Pym and a saved young theological student, Ben, arrive.

Jacob's mother elects to take this opportunity to discuss the essential humanity of Christ while waiting for Brenda to make a last-minute excursion to the loo.

'Excreta, do you see, explain it all,' she points out to the student of divinity.

Ben manufactures a cough; swivels his eyes to the top shelf of a bookcase, at which he squints. Normally I would see it as my duty to cut off May's excursus before it could develop into fullblown apostasy but today I make no intervention.

'Jesus had to empty his bowels same as us. Did he not, young man, I'm talking to you.'

'Of course the Bible is not explicit on these scatological matters,' states Ben through his beard, behind his hand.

'It draws a veil,' adds Miss Pym. 'Wisely.'

'So you don't believe Jesus was human?' she beetle-brows them.

'Yes of course – that's the whole point.'

'And humans shit?'

'Well . . .'

'They do or they don't?'

'Yes, but . . .'

'Ergo, young man, Christ *shat*. Each man hath in him the power to create seventy times seven tons of waste matter in thirty-three years. And an entire lake of piss.

That is what being human is all about. Did Adam have a BTM?'

Murmurings.

'Exactly. Of course he did. And for what?' she catechises.

No reply.

'And if Adam, then so too the second Adam. And where did he shit?'

No volunteers.

'Well, obviously, behind rocks or in sundry other convenient places. Which we now know as conveniences.'

Deborah mutters that it's not strictly relevant, dear.

'Oh – really – *not strictly relevant dear*,' May mimes. 'Are you aware of the massive volume of cattle-farts that are at this minute destroying the ozone layer? I suppose that's not strictly relevant either?'

Sucking busily on her lips, she enquires of Miss Pym if this young man is a hypocrite?

'Oh no,' says Pym breathlessly. 'Ben is a saved soul, May, and stands up to testify at all the meetings – and obeyed a divine leading by springing up on to a bench on Pride Hill and speaking to the shoppers and office people last Friday afternoon, between the Town Cross and Burger King – '

'But he denies his BTM. So he must be a hypocrite. Or a fool.'

'Poor dear May,' whispers Miss Pym to me, when Brenda has finally climbed into her chair. 'Alzheimer's is it? I hadn't realised she was getting so . . .'

Miss Pym and Ben carry on up the Cop and Dogpole as we four turn off for the river. May exclaims that the air is instantly fresher, 'less farty by far'.

She calls out 'Cow parsley!', 'Dock!' and 'Thistles' as she spots them on the river bank, for she is partial to weeds and laments the Council scythes that lay the green world low. Brenda and Peter are discussing the kingfishers they've seen in past years on the Severn and the Rea Brook. They speak of the pair of sedge warblers reliably sighted last year, visiting Shrewsbury from Africa; the secret salmon spawning on the shingle banks of the Rea Brook; otters passing through.

'Meadowsweet... soft rush... moorhens, sandmartins' I hear them chorus, their voices slightly raised, as if to persuade me that amidst all the despoliation, there is a work of salvage going on behind the scenes. 'Whitethroats... siskin... kingfishers, kingfishers.'

Birdsong; young breeze-breathed leaves the light lifts through; spanglings on olive water... I take in all this, conscious that it is to comfort me that these two preach the gospel of kingfishers.

I try to be comforted and to merit their warmth, conscious of having failed Brenda, Nathan and May, uncomfortably aware that I may well repeat the offence; self-proclaimed Samaritan fallen sick by the wayside.

As we walk through the clemency of milky spring light, a growth swells in me, alongside the grief and shock, fed by the grief and shock. What surgery will remove such malignancy? I've little conscious acquaintance with anger, except against cruelty and injustice outside my own walls. Apartheid, genocide, torture, poverty, these raised rage: but a clean anger, which led me to bear witness alongside tender-hearted people on darkening street-corners, swinging candles in jamjars; standing in solidarity with Christ against moneychangers, Pharisees, Caesar. Then I'd come home to my indoor round of ministering where I belonged, where I was happy. It was a life of witness; a sacramental life.

Today, silently pushing Jacob's mother up the gently

bosomy slope of the Quarry, I see there was no virtue in it. I was cloistered. I was never tempted.

Now I'm living where so many other people have to live.

Such a peculiar feeling of guilt. Looking back, I can clearly see all the times Jacob came in and I allowed myself to be rushed off my feet; failed to greet him with more than a skimmed kiss, skimped enquiry as to how his day had been. Haring upstairs with piles of ironing, saying 'Could you just get your own meal out of the oven, there's a dear?' Listening to May's prattle when I should have been attending to him. Putting everything before my husband's needs.

My face always in shadow, turned away. Always plumping someone's pillow or pulling someone's bedsocks on. Fixated on sleep because I knew it was likely I'd be up in the night at least twice. This inattention would open the door and let the blonde woman in.

But I did it all for you! Jacob, I did it for you!

I'm starting to feel distaste for people; catch myself thinking vindictive thoughts about them. Listening to May chomping her food this morning nauseated me. Now, as we enter the Dingle, and Peter calls Catherine's scampering children 'Little dears', the odious suspicion is spawned that Peter, dear Peter, good kind Peter, might not be all he seems. What's he covering up for, making a profession of walking ancient ladies along river banks and shepherding people with learning difficulties on jaunts to Ellesmere Port? Some perversion, some retardation.

For if Jacob, then Peter.

All my life I've known Jacob as a good man. For decades I've accepted Peter as dear and harmless. When he stopped and spoke so sweetly to the lads with their toy fishing nets, I thought of pederast-priests, I detected a sick leer stealing over his face.

I saw a film of my own projecting.

For if Jacob, if Peter, then Jessie: Jessie, whose mind is minute by minute curdling, corrupting, so that she generates phantom images of her own conception.

It's a good thing I never had children; people like me should never breed.

Look what you're doing to me, Jacob, I blaze.

The Dingle glows yellow like a light-source: daffodils and primroses mass like blessings in our sight.

'I want to sit down on my parents,' insists May eagerly.

'Of course you shall,' I say, and she is eased from the chair to the bench in memory of her parents:

IN MEMORY OF JACOB AND ANNA PURVIS

'Put my cushion right, Dee Dee. It's all on the tilt here.'

Around the lopsided basin of the flower garden, elderly people bask on the benches, women read books. Couples drift, leaving brief trails of vowels hanging in the air – Border Welsh, Wolverhampton, BBC, Midlands. May's strict parents turned to wood are honoured, as she puts it, by her posterior.

Rhododendrons pool, purple, white, and an amazing tangerine. The fountain plays into the greenly shadowed water.

May remarks that it makes her want to pee.

IN MEMORY OF CYRIL LATIMER 1896–1973 AND JESSIE LATIMER 1899–1990 TOGETHER AGAIN, reads the plaque on a bench near the exit. I turn my head away from that other Jessie who after seventeen years of vigil could legitimately expect to go home to her mate.

Joe snoozes in his buggy, his nose bubbling with a freshly caught cold, head sunk into his shoulders so that his cheeks are red pouches. He looks oddly old as he slumps there at May's feet; and May's hankering after the wishing well, in the Shoemakers' Arbour, has a child-like eagerness.

'Come on, you make a wish, Dee Dee,' she urges, as we stare through the wrought-iron gate to the crumbling sandstone vase, 'make a wish and I'll treat you.'

Ivy creeps around the decayed heads of St Crispin and St Crispian, patron saints of shoemakers, the lower part of whose legs have fallen off with time, so that we cannot assess the fashion of their footwear.

'You wish for me,' I say, and she makes a long, muttered wish to the value of ten pence, which lies at the root of the crumbled fountain amongst crisp packets and mouldered leaves.

'There you are. You should be all right now.'

She then engages in a wrestle with the Borough gardeners, who have come with a hand-drawn trolley to cull the yellow-and-white flowers of spring, still in their prime, and replace them with a geometrical arrangement of scarlet summer bedding plants. The gardeners explain that you have to get rid of the old flowers when they're past their sell-by date.

'But they're not dying,' May complains. 'It's a waste, it's a crying shame', and is denouncing the gardeners as vandals and Salop as a fascist state (she will escape to Wrekin when it secedes from the County Council) when Peter hastily suggests that we visit Sabrina in her fountain to see how she's getting on, and maybe share out the kingsize bar of fruit and nut he's brought.

'Chocolate binds you up something dreadful,' May observes, chewing vigorously, and roves back to the Holy Land and the theological turn of mind which I had hoped she'd left at home. 'Do you suppose Jesus ever suffered from constipation, Peter? . . . Possibly not, even though he was human, because of high fibre diet, *with* grit (sand, you see, from the desert) and also perhaps the figs which as you may or may not know, Peter, but, Brenda as a geographer you assuredly will know, are plentiful in that part of the world, and have a similar effect to prunes – so he may have escaped that particular curse, also, for obvious reasons, childbirth.'

'Oh, do look at the rhododendron island, May dear,' says Brenda. 'What a picture.'

'When we get home,' May states, 'I shall eat seven prunes. Just to be on the safe side.'

She will not easily forget the foolish young hospital nurse who once spooned twenty-two into her at one sitting; and the long-term seismic effects thereof, which she now begins to specify.

If she says one more word about bowels, I shall scream an almighty and apocalyptic scream.

'I can't stand it,' I tell Catherine, nails digging into the palms of my hands. 'I can't stand it. I can't.'

Cathy and I leave all our dependants in Peter's willing hands and climb out of the Dingle. I explain to her as we go how I can no longer cope with May; it is, she is, more than I can bear.

'I – just – can't – *bear* – it – another moment,' I keep snarling.

'I couldn't either. I don't know how you've managed,' says Cathy, squeezing my arm.

Leaving through the blue Quarry gates, we linger at the balustrade overlooking the park at a blessed distance from where my husband's mother is blasting away at the top of her voice, beyond our hearing. Light shimmers in soft trees beyond trees; new-mown grass scent rises like a pagan incense.

'I've had enough,' I tell her. 'She maddens me.'

'Poor Jessie. Can't the Social Services give you more help? Surely they will, now that . . .'

'I shouldn't think so.'

'Then you must put her in a home.'

'Oh, I couldn't do that,' I come in quickly, heart clenching tight. A cold cloud comes down on me.

'Why not though, honestly?'

'Oh, I couldn't live with myself.'

'But she'd be okay, Jessie, when she'd got used to it. If you chose somewhere good. And you could visit her every other day, or something like that . . . quality time. You deserve . . . a life.' As she counsels me in a voice of reason, with upbeat cadences, I withdraw progressively from her, into a feeling of loveless, lame inertia she could never imagine. Cathy seems younger than myself by more than her actual four years. She belongs with the young and procreative; I have stepped over into the shadows, shackled. Her young will shed their down and fly the nest; my charges will shrivel, slowly, as I age, my living body tied to their degeneration.

'No,' I reply. 'No. I can't.'

'But why, love?'

'Because . . . because I'm programmed that way.'

I begin to walk, stiffly, rather fast, into the vertiginous shadow of the dome of Chad's, as if I were splitting up from my self.

She is on my heels.

'You don't need to be programmed. You can choose a life of your own.'

'I'd rather die.'

She cannot understand the apprehension of public and private worthlessness; I'd feel skinned alive, flayed. Ditching May as I have been ditched.

Yet it is true I cannot stand her any longer.

'I don't understand.'

'I know you don't.'

'Well, I do, Jessie, I do of course, but I wish you'd get out of your mind-set.'

I do not retort with the angry words that leap to mind, *My mind-set is me*, but lurch round in the lee of this building, darkened by pollution, which threatens to topple on me, the great dome vertiginously stacked with cube, polygon, cone, the complex argument of a tectonics surmounted by the heavy imperative of the Cross.

But when we are inside, there is a world of Palladian domed whiteness that opens out vistas to my trapped spirit. Two tiers of galleries describe circles within circles, white above, brown below; on both levels gold-topped fluted columns, Ionic and Corinthian, are planted like the graceful essences of trees to create the sense of a temple. It is the still coolness that speaks to me. Not God's love or his alien majesty. Pure light and space, almost abstracted.

Catherine moves towards the altar; I watch her from where I sit. Last Harvest Festival we came, she being pregnant, and found a touching little trove of Worcester Permains, Cheshire potatoes, a grapefruit, a leek, an orange and a little pile of conkers at the base of the font, which held an unopened packet of six Mars bars. At the elegant base of each pillar was arranged an offering of apples. A month later when we came to an organ recital, we found one overlooked apple still in place, wrinkled and faintly cider-smelling in the cool air.

Now Cathy lights a candle amongst others in a trough of sand before the altar; her fair hair silvered by light falling through the round-arched window. My eye rests on Catherine standing there, finds rest in the quiet she stands and breathes, her full breasts rising and falling, the shadowed folds of her dove-grey skirt swaying slightly. She steadies me by simply existing in my line of sight.

'You are so dear and lovely, Cathy,' I whisper, coming up behind her and laying one arm gently round her waist. 'And I love you, and I'm so glad of you.'

The candle-flame reflects in the tear upon the pupil of Cathy's eye as she turns to me.

We lace hands and, almost as if this were an ordinary day rather than the end of my world, stroll round the curving walls of the nave, marvelling not for the first time at how worthy were the Shrewsbury worthies of the last century, magistrates' clerks, mayors, physicians, architects: 'irreproachable integrity', 'exemplary conduct as a husband and father', 'affable and benevolent'. The few women represented all apparently practised the identical virtues, of 'patience' and 'pious humility'.

We hear our dear ones squalling from outside the Dingle, which, as we approach, assumes the dimensions of a giant playpen, keeping our charges' mayhem within some bounds. Peter in his shirt-sleeves is anxiously cradling a bawling Joe, who has awoken feverish and maddened with mother-loss. Zeke is up a small tree, having scaled the pool-railings to attain it. Brenda has snared Catherine's screaming middle son by the dungarees and looks ready to faint.

'Oh glory,' says Cathy, as she begins the work of salvage, 'here we go.'

'So where have you two herberts been?' demands May.

I kiss her hectic cheek.

'Just mooching round Chad's, dear. I'm sorry: were we long?'

'Long? You were hours. Everything's gone to pot.'

'Sorry, love.'

'And hours.'

'Well, I'm back now.'

'Oh are you, missus. Well, I need to go to the loo so look sharp. And that old blighter Brother Cadfael has been in here with his fellow monks. Look, there they are now – over there.'

'Who?'

'It's Nathan, Jessie,' says Brenda. 'They're having a little outing.'

And there is my uncle, sitting with a group of his fellow residents in the balmy spring air, shepherded by a bevy of youthful care-workers.

'The old crackpot says he hears the beating of the wings of the Holy Spirit outside his window,' scoffs May. 'I told him it was more likely the pigeons.'

Nathan tells me about his move to a private room; how matron came in and said, 'Your niece thinks you'll be happier on your own, Mr Copplestone'; how they bustled him through, his personal property conveyed in two grey binbags, while Mr Jones was away playing cards in the day-room.

He sat for a long while thinking of Jonah and the whale, hardly able to restrain the tears of relief. He laid out comb, brush, and clothes-brush on the embroidered cloth on the dressing table. When Mr Jones had come to visit, he said there was no room to swing a cat. But at his age, Nathan pointed out, one does not need to charge about; just a little light pottering will suffice. Plainness facilitates prayer and contemplation, and there is a sufficiently ascetic view over the drainpiped rear of the building, including a jumble of dustbins and a segment of car park.

'Well, if you're happy with it, love?'

'I am happy and most thankful. I cannot tell you what

it meant to me to have a room of my own. Of course, it is a little pink, being really a lady's room. It is thought that ladies prefer pastel shades which I suppose in general they do – do they? But anyhow if someone could bring my old white candlewick, it would be an enhancing detail. At your convenience, dear.'

'Are you really more settled now?'

'Oh, yes. You see, I like my privacy. Mr Jones was an unusually genial man, but it's late in the day for me to learn to share. He was a talker, and we hadn't a great deal in common. Barmaids seemed to be his favourite topic and, being teetotal, I have little experience of such. Now of course Paul and Silas had to share a prison-cell, I've no quarrel with the principle of doubling up, but I confess it is a relief to enjoy the peace of a sanctum.'

Cathy and I can imagine that such peace may be rather qualified. Slippered feet surely traipse the corridor; quavering, long-drawn cries distress the ears; and women peer in as they wander in their confusion up and down, up and down the corridor. Perhaps the loquacious company of Mr Jones is a necessary preliminary to appreciation of the peace he's found.

'Are you sure,' he asks me, 'the extra can be afforded?'

'Don't you worry about that.'

Also he has a new friend: Dorothy, a fellow spirit; a Quaker.

'Any news . . .?' he asks.

I tell him the news.

'I was afraid so,' is all he says, without surprise, so that I fancy he knew in advance obvious things that entirely escaped me for twenty years.

Chapter 7

Ludlow was sabbath afternoons browsing bookshops, meandering the cobbled alleys arm-in-arm and saying *So you've not fallen down yet* to our favourite ancient buildings. Jacob would contemplate the medieval houses with a carpenter's fellow-feeling for the old masons' methods and materials. He'd read them aloud to me like books. And once he so forgot his shy reserve as to stand in the middle of the street measuring out with gestures of his hands the scarcely tenable angles and extensions of an ancient house in King Street, as to attract a knot of listeners who took him for a tour-guide.

And there he stood, where I stand now, enlarging to me on mitre joints, mortises, dove-tailing, joists, laths and studs . . . a tall, dark-haired man in his prime, surrounded, so it seemed, by American golfers in white shoes and flat caps.

'Is that so?' breathed one. 'But how simply fascinating . . .'

And they began to point and speculate as to why the house had not succeeded in falling long ago, sagging sideways and toppling forward, on a sloped road where every house seemed to have tackled the acute gradient by electing to lean in a different direction.

'And are you, sir, may I ask, an architect?'

'Heck, no, I'm just a joiner.'

'A – who?'

'A carpenter – well, really, a man of all work,' said Jacob, colouring up, while a camera flash fixed him in celluloid, a keepsake for Miami; and a pang of pride went through my chest. I stepped up, linked arms and told them he was a craftsman in the old tradition.

'And do you have a shop?'

No: just his hands and tools.

Disappointment: if the craftsman had owned a shop, they'd all have piled in and bought up Jacob's wares. He seemed transparently the real thing.

'Honestly, Jessie, what did you have to go and say that for?' he asked, head down, making off to a quiet corner of De Grey's Café.

'Say what?'

'About being a craftsman?'

'Because it's true, that's why.'

I loved his crumpled corduroy modesty; his listening air; the way he looked everyone directly in the eye and gave a straight answer.

I am not able to eat until I have seen him again. When he has looked me in the eye and said that he is no longer Jacob, then I'll begin to believe he can have left me.

Strange how rigidly calm I felt on Shrewsbury Station, waiting for the Cardiff train, something like my mental state before my librarianship exams all those years ago, a choked trance. In this calm I glided between the Stretton hills, past the black-and-white Herefords in the fields where sheep are lambing, to disembark at Ludlow and cross the worn steps of the old railway bridge. Past Upper Galdeford, the Tudor houses are a migraineur's nightmare of black-and-white busyness; I pass queasily through smells of fishmonger and bakery.

In the marketplace, above the entrance to Quality

Square stands a venerable brick-built house we thought of as pregnant: its middle bulges out, braced by a corset of iron girders and two elliptical black bolts. The structure holds itself together by sucking in its breath at the windows, to restrain its sagging belly. How often we've stood in the Square holding hands and marvelling at its resistance to attrition and gravity. *So you're still with us.*

Netley Road is Georgian, elegant, a terrace of ochre, cream, russet façades, where people live behind net curtains, their doors beautified by hanging baskets of geraniums and ivies. I don't recall this road at all, happening into it before the street-map seems to indicate I should, like a street that awaits you in a dream. Yet everything here is neutral, genteel, in a setting where trauma and eros would be alike alien. A man up a ladder who is not Jacob is banging at a sash window towards the far end where the blue-green hills show through.

At Jacob's rented jade green door, I am unable to knock. In the sudden ebb of confidence, I find myself retreating to a narrow back passageway behind the terrace, yielding a view down over its nether regions and small rectangular back gardens. I count my way along to Number 19. Prowling the hindquarters of their lodging, trespassing by the garden of my husband's infidelity, in perhaps the most undignified action of my life, I squint over a low wall at the washing line on which Jacob's underwear is hanging, definitely his, the pants and socks I buy him from Marks and Spencer; also thin, gauzy bras ... and there are children's clothes too – little dresses and Micky Mouse T-shirts.

That is the bad, the bruising sight: Jacob's new children's vulnerable garments exposed to my sick eye. I back away; post a note through the door telling

Jacob I shall be at De Grey's till six and would he come and talk to me?

The long, low-ceilinged room, like a sepia print, dissolves in a brown dusk of filtered light the leavings of the past. Nothing changes here from uneven floorboards to brown beams, old tables and chairs that were the same as when Mother had brought me for treats of tea-cakes, lemonade with a blob of ice-cream fizzing in it. Even the elderly waitresses seem immortal. There's a kind of settled dullness over everything. My bladder aches to be emptied but I'm scared to disappear in case he comes and misses me.

Things continue. That's what I assumed. Traditions; generations; indissoluble bonds and bondings. They neither lapse nor snap with time if you plait them firmly enough.

We'd built our house on rock, not sand. I'd felt ourselves supported from beneath; the two of us; the family; the fellowship of the church; the founding promises of Christ; the Bible open beneath us, its pages parted at the spine, gold-edged, believable, life-guaranteeing – the twin halves of the book supporting our vows at every turn.

Evidently Jacob hadn't felt the same.

Or perhaps he had shared my belief for nineteen years and in the twentieth shifted.

I cannot stop thinking about bras pruriently spied on a washing line; young breasts, firm, taut, proudly perfect.

A blonde. Dyed? Perhaps it's dyed.

From the sublimity of Bible promises, I have sunk so suddenly to the unworthy compensations of ill-wishing.

Get a grip. Remember who you are.

The sex was no good . . . you said that . . . no good.

Forget . . . erase that.

I trace with a heavy knife a complex line between the stains and blemishes on the faded tablecloth. The more forensically I examine it, the more apparent become the shadings of residual stains endless relaundering only ploughs in deeper.

An apparently limitless supply of Welsh ladies marches along the single strip of carpet in and out of the ladies' toilet. Tedium of everlasting chairs creaking on floorboards.

As I stand up to leave, Jacob enters.

From another world, he comes in.

Then it is embarrassed matter-of-fact for a few minutes: he asks am I hungry? and orders tea for two and tea-cakes. I say I don't want anything to eat. He says okay, whatever I can't manage, he'll finish.

He taps a cigarette on the table-cloth. His hands are quivering, his beautiful hands. I stare at the cigarette: 'But I didn't think . . . you smoked.'

'Only Silk Cut,' he says, with a rueful twist of the mouth. 'Low Tar.'

'But how long have you . . .?' It pains me to see him gasp that filth into his lungs, pour out pollution in a long exhalation, his head turned away from me. Brenda knew. She said you could smell it on his breath. I assumed the smokiness was breathed on to him by others.

'I occasionally have one on the job, that's all.'

'Ah. I didn't realise.'

I study my tea-cup, with a sense of dawning recognition: myself fussing, bustling round after visitors have been in with a pipe or cigarette, pushing up the sash to let in fresh air. An expression of unendurable patience on my face (I can see it now, as if in a mirror, how I must have looked) giving way to indignation as I shoot up the sash to admit the purifying gale. I blush to remember these houseproud reflexes.

'Well, never mind,' Jacob soothes. He would always conciliate. 'I'll stub it out if you can't stand it. It's the stress.'

But he doesn't stub it out. He continues to consume the smoke as if life itself depended on filling his airways with it.

When the tea comes, Jacob waits for me to pour.

Having waited, he wonders, 'Aren't you going to pour?'

'No, I don't think so,' I say. 'It's your turn.'

Jacob hands me a cup of tea. He never made me cups of tea, Nathan said.

'Can I beg a cigarette?' I ask.

'But you don't smoke.' He looks faintly shocked.

'I do now.'

He bites into his tea-cake without further comment, as I battle with the choking effects of the cigarette, the first of my life.

Then he wolfs my tea-cake.

'Are you okay, Jessie?' he asks, hopefully. 'I've been bothered about you. I'd have got in touch, you know. You needn't have felt you had to . . . come over.'

He looks furtively uneasy.

'But, Jacob, why run away?'

'Well, I'm not, Jessie, but there are . . . other people to take into consideration . . . and I'm really anxious to keep the temperature down. For everyone's sake.'

His eyes narrow. Is he calculating some ratio, balancing myself and the Oldies against Hazel and the youngsters? I magnify those eyes as if in close-up: curl of lash, dilated pupil, familiar wrinkles and laughter-lines. Impossible to believe you could not want to reach out to me as I faint to reach out to you, and touch, and hold, and laugh, and say 'It was all a delusion, a bad dream, there was only ever you.'

'*Jacob*,' I remonstrate.

'I know ... I know. I'm sorry. I've nil excuses. But could you let me, sort of, organise things this end, Jessie? Not come running after me. You see, it's quite bad for Hazel to get upset.'

'Really?'

'Yes, I worry for her nerves.'

'*Her* nerves?'

He sails on to explain that whereas I'm strong and capable, Hazel is made of very fragile, fine stuff; I'd understand if I met her; and she's had a rotten life. In a queer sort of way, he adds, and a sliver of light gleams in my mind, she reminds him of Nella.

'And what about your ... our ... relatives?'

Ah, well, he shifts in his seat and thrusts his hands deep in his jacket pockets: ah well. He reminds me that he's never exactly got on with his mother; I was the only one who could handle her.

'We are still responsible for them,' I remind him.

'Presumably you'll ... want to ... go on caring for them?'

'I'm not thinking of forsaking them.' I pledge myself with righteous rage to an open-ended term of imprisonment.

And my husband, at last seeing or acknowledging my disfiguring anger, replies: 'Don't be narked, Jessie.'

Narked. Had he always spoken like that, diminishingly, stupidly, shamefully?

'I feel I've never known you,' I tell him, breaking up the crust of brown sugar in the bowl and stirring it with the spoon.

'Perhaps there isn't that much to know,' he suggested. 'Perhaps I'm just an ordinary sort of chap.'

Higgamus hoggamus, Brenda's voice alerts me with its cryptic wisdom. *Hoggamus higgamus*.

'Would you just tell me, Jacob,' I ask gently, 'were there other women before Hazel?'

'Not . . . really,' he mumbles.

I enquire no further. I sit back; take a deep breath. Apparently we belong to adjacent but foreign tribes, whose languages are only superficially alike. Looking round the restaurant at the scattering of couples at tables, I wonder if all of us shared this language difficulty; this *higgamus hoggamus* dilemma? Most of the couples are not speaking; have long ago dispensed all that they wished to communicate. Now they glance idly round the walls, sharing their ruminant silence. In a corner, two middle-aged women twitter like birds. Otherwise there are only Jacob and myself locked in an engagement of *higgamus* with *hoggamus*.

Or so I thought.

But then Jacob says, 'Look, Jessie, I won't beat about the bush. It's not fair on you.'

His eyes, that have been narrowed and hooded, become the eyes of the candid Jacob whose integrity I would have died to assert.

'Yes?' I said, to help him on; to bring him back to himself and to me. 'Go on, love. I'll listen.'

'Well, I'm not sure if you've guessed, but Hazel's going to have a baby – our baby. And that . . . really does change everything . . . and it's split my loyalties right down the middle. Oh – Jessie – *Jessie* – I'm so, so sorry. I wouldn't have had this happen for the world.'

'No, now, Jacob, love, it's all right, it's all right. No, I'll be all right. Now that I know,' and my eyes brim but the scalding tears are also healing; because he has tight hold of both my hands and he is weeping too across the table; and I say, 'Jacob, it will be all right, I will make it all right, I promise.'

Oh, and as he unlooses his hold of my hands, I keel back into the country of loss. He's going back to her. He rips off me like a layer of skin. I sway where I stand, melted with longing. One kiss: I dare not ask for it but my eyes supplicate: one kiss.

He has no kisses for me. Instead he offers praise for my sterling qualities.

'You're such a generous woman, Jessie. I'm so grateful.'

He settles the bill.

'I really am grateful.'

'Well,' I say as we falter in Broad Street outside the cafe, 'now that I understand ... I can maybe sort-of stretch to include your new family in my ... love and care. After all, as you say, Hazel' (how that name scorches me to say) 'has suffered, and she deserves our ... fellow-feeling. Would you tell her from me, Jacob, that, in her own time, I should be glad to meet her and welcome her and the little ones ... in all love and charity.' That sounds a false note; I hurry to restore the tune. 'No, I don't mean that as it sounds – I don't mean to be pi – '

'Of course not, you're just being your wonderful, caring self,' he lip-services me. I swallow hard.

'No – no; please don't put it like that. What I need is to salvage some ... meaning ... out of all this. Not to throw away a lifetime of love and devotion. I do know how much you wanted babies, Jacob ... and I couldn't give you even one.'

Jacob shifts from foot to foot as if the pavement were red-hot. His eyes blink with each relocation of balance.

He thanks me again; promises to get in touch, and I vow in return to keep away until contacted or summoned.

'You are an amazing woman, Jessie,' he assures me. 'There can't be another woman in the world who would have taken a thing like this as you have.'

Kiss me: only kiss me. I look from his eyes to his lips, and see the tenderness of the skin, slightly swollen, from sex with her that has made him realise that the sex had never been any good between us. But I'd have been so happy to learn, I tell him silently, why didn't you think to teach me – if you knew? My womb stirs as I study the skin of his lips, the tiny scar beneath his underlip, and all the while I generously hand him over to the unknown lady with the fair hair.

With mine own hands I give away my crown,
With mine own tears I wash away my balm.

He doesn't kiss me. When he notices the direction of my eyes, he rubs at his chin and underlip, as if thinking I'd detected some crumb or fleck of blood from shaving. He must be so used to my finicking over tidiness.

'Well then,' my husband says to his wife. 'I'll be in touch – very shortly.'

'Perhaps we could set a time,' I suggest in a briskly practical manner. 'So that I can pick up the phone on the upstairs extension.'

'Good thinking. I don't know if I'm up to coping with any more of mum's carry-on at the moment. Honestly, Jess, I don't know how you stand it. I don't want to be unkind but the *relief* of not having to listen to that . . . jabbering prattle. I know I shouldn't say it.'

I wish he had not reverted to that sheepishly coarse way of speaking, seeing me as a convenience, to cope with his rejects. I take a step back.

'Perhaps, in your own time, you'll feel more able to come and speak to May?' I prompt quietly. 'She's suffering quite a lot – but she shows it in her own way. Until then, of course I'll take care of her and Brenda in the best way I can.'

Jacob's tenterhooks pavement-dancing begins again. He fiddles with his watch-strap; grimaces nervously, his face angled aside, in so odd a manner that a passer-by stops, thinking Jacob is trying to button-hole him.

'Do I know you?' asks the shopper.

'No,' says Jacob. 'I'd best be on my way,' he tells me. 'Hazel will be worrying.'

'Of course.'

I kiss him lightly on the cheek and he flees.

Odd how, on the train, I keep thinking of Nella.

I wonder how she is; what kind of a life she is leading. She'll be nearly nineteen years old now.

Tempestuous girl with a wilderness of uncombable tawny hair. Storm of rushing skirts speeding past me down the staircase, shouting 'Tadpoles! Tadpoles!' Life, life unquenchable, even after all the blows she'd been dealt by that tender age. All these years I'd yearned for her. Several times I wrote to Social Services at Shirehall requesting her address, but her 'real' mother vetoed a meeting between myself and her child. I could understand that jealousy.

Perhaps one day I'll see you, Nella. I'll say, trying to be calm, ordinary, 'How have you been, love, all these years?'

If Nella had never been taken away, she'd have become priority. We'd not have taken in the Old Ones; at least in such numbers; Jacob would surely still be with me?

The train strikes into spectacular cloven weather:

storm-clouds mass in one half of the sky against the last of the sunshine in the other. A farmhouse on the Long Mynd is blanched against charcoal clouds, orange-gold reflections burning on its panes. Sheep and lambs are whitewashed in the pasture; and the new green is goldened by the strange light.

If Nella came to me, I'd know her at once. Thin gazelle legs in white ankle-socks canter away into the past. She'd come to me erect and shapely, her face still long and narrow, grey-green eyes pensive, as she could be when not dashing around helter-skelter. I hope they've not tamed Nella as they've neutered me, I find myself thinking . . .

. . . neutered? What a peculiar word to apply to myself. No, her wildness was a sign of damage. Surely it was.

I'll bash you with these nettles, she once said, advancing with a fistful held in a bunch of dockleaves. *I will so, I'll thrash you*. And she actually did flip me with them, on my bare forearm. Then she cried to see the rash come up and plastered me with dock-leaves. I didn't reproach her. All the way home on the bus, she clung, whining for sweets. Not wanting to see my arm, with its external confirmation of her own inner trouble.

If you're damaged, you do inevitably pass it on. I comprehended that rule quite clearly when we fostered her. I fully expected to be attacked with nettles.

But I won't pass on my damage. No, Jacob, no. I swell with uneasy pride and sit taller in my seat, determining to grow greater through all this, and doesn't all growth hurt? If I can straighten my spine and reach out beyond my own pain . . . we'll all be bonded together in one loving group . . . all of us together. There need never be any feeling of loss if I can just stretch my sympathy far enough . . .

The young man in the leather jacket sitting opposite is observing me with a trace of amusement. I realise I'm puffing my chest out like a pouter pigeon, holding a huge breath. My tenderness is alloyed with cunning negotiation. I let out the breath; turn my head aside to the deflated shadow of a woman in the pane, at once wild-eyed, defiled and calculating.

I focus my entire attention upon May; I call her darling and sweetheart, and make it appear that my entire object in life is to promote her well-being. This was how I used to live: surely I should be able to pick up the lost loving rhythms again?

The blandishments, the cherishings, these used to come as a matter of course, along with the listening air, which now I feign. But May, as she has often told me, is a member of the intelligentsia who could have gone to university to study, if anybody had thought so to privilege her, and can spot a fake coming from a mile off. She is having none of it. Sequesters herself in dignified silence in response to my wheedlings and denotes her awareness of my existence only by swivellings of the eye.

Tired of it, tired of her, I dump myself on the settee and my pulse drums to think of Jacob now in Ludlow with his arm round Hazel, a blue-eyed child on his knee.

I must draw them from the hinterland of fantasy into the light of day. They won't scare me when I see they're solidly human and just as vulnerable as I am. In the real world I'll be able to embrace Hazel as a friend.

'Whatever you want to do is, I'm sure, the right thing,' says Brenda mildly, as I lift her legs into bed to settle her for the night. 'This blinking collar, I just can't get it right.' Her fingers fidget ineffectually at the soft collar in which she sleeps. We fight the collar for a while; then we fight the pillows, to prop her painful neck at the appropriate angle, a tricky manoeuvre since the osteoporosis humped Brenda's back. She will die, as we both know, of lung-compression, her head forced progressively down to her chest until she can no longer breathe; that's unless a friendly heart-attack carries her off in her sleep; the substance of her nightly *Nunc dimittis*. I slough my own woes in pondering the difficulty of her journey.

Perched on the edge of the bed, I tenderly smooth her high forehead free of tension. With both hands I massage the temples and say, 'You have a good night now, Brennie, no worries. You've done enough, what with putting up with me having multiple hysterics.'

'Mmm,' she closes her eyes. 'That's lovely, Jess – most soothing.'

Brenda is so much easier to love than May. Perhaps if I begin with her and work along?

'So tedious for you,' she apologises.

'Not a bit. I just wish there were more we could do for your comfort. Do you want me to get the geriatrician in again to have a look at you?'

'No, Jessie. Let be. I might lie up for a day or two if you don't mind. The Dingle took it out of me, I have to admit.'

Her pain can be searing at this time of day. I refill her water-jug with ice-cubes.

'Can you reach, love? Have you everything you need for the night?'

'Yes; now you get some rest,' she urges. 'I've been thinking we ought to have a nurse in at night for May. You desperately need rest.'

'Perhaps Social Services will come up with something, I'll ring them,' I suggest, marvelling at how far I have abdicated my role as all-sufficient saviour, who needed neither sleep nor physical help with my burden.

'Doubt it,' murmurs Brenda. 'They're cutting everything.'

'She's a touch nervous,' confides Jacob over the phone, 'about meeting you – but I've told her the gist of what you said about understanding and welcoming her and so forth. I've explained to her what a strong person you are and a Christian, and so you're not – you know, like other wives might be in your place – vindictive. Well, Jessie,' he gallops on, 'I do know you're hurt. I mean, *I* know that. But there's no point in . . . you know . . . rubbing it in to *her*. I mean, it's between the two of us, that part, isn't it?

'Of course,' I concur, while the Health Visitor (not the one May took against and punched) is conducting a conversation with Jacob's mother to determine the extent of her frailties both mental and physical.

As the health visitor goes clicking out on her high heels, looking fazed and dishevelled, and commenting, 'She's an unusual lady, isn't she? So terribly imaginative,' social services draws up with a screech of brakes. Social services dives in and whips round, examining domestic arrangements, explaining that she has three other visits to get through before lunch-time, it's no joke, she's desperate to take early retirement and purchase a nice little bungalow in Baschurch. She seems oblivious to May's cries of 'Who's this nosy old bag now? What's she want?'

Mrs Teague suggests a couple of gadgets that might come in handy and ventures the name of a private care service, enquiring as to the amount of May's savings. May caustically explains to her that she is a millionairess, having won the lottery rollover only last week.

'Shameless hussy, coming round here wanting a hand-out!'

'Goodness me, no, dear,' says Mrs Teague. 'I am just assessing your eligibility, Mrs Copplestone . . .'.

'*When* we need help be assured we shall ask for it,' states May grandly.

'Well, your daughter-in-law *has* requested . . .'

'Nonsense. Dee Dee is quite able-bodied – strong as a carthorse. As anyone with eyes can see. Perhaps you suffer from an ophthalmic disorder, young woman, in which case I can recommend eyewash for your hogwash.'

'Right then, I'll be off,' says Mrs Teague, bouncing up.

'Jessie, it's me again.' Jacob rings back in a hail-fellow voice. 'Sorry to keep pestering you when I know you must be busy.'

'We've just had the health visitor and social services,' I said.

'Why, what's happened?'

'Nothing. I just need help, that's all.'

'Oh. Ah.'

'Anyway they've gone now.'

'Ah. Right. Well, not to beat about the bush, what I wondered was, can we set a time to come and visit? Hazel and I have been talking things out, we've had a nice long chat, and we want to put something to you . . . see if we can sort things out in a . . . civilised way. I said I was sure you would be open to any idea that would make things happier for everybody, including her.'

'Yes indeed. When are you coming?'

'Oh – tomorrow suit you? . . . Right. I'd better let you get back to it then.'

The District Nurse rings. She can't come to assess us

this week after all, sorry about that, and anyway it's not an emergency. They may be able to send someone next week.

CHAPTER 8

Mist wreathes the river and floats up round the shrubs in swathes. Fuzzy lights on the opposite bank come and go like hazy suspicions; and all sound is muffled, as if the suspicions went unacknowledged. I have awakened knowing that crowds of lies have been admitted to my house over a period of years, coming in bare-faced through the front door, smiling straight into my eyes from the armchair. When I open the porch door to bring in the milk, the reek of traffic fumes caught up in the mist reminds me of smoke from the cigarettes I never knew Jacob smoked.

Didn't I know? Was I that dense? Surely I must have caught and surreptitiously denied the staleness on his breath? I did sometimes cotton on to an odour of the not-quite-right, but Jacob must have been an expert in covering up – pulling a face and complaining before I did about the dangers of passive smoking.

Perhaps they won't come in this fog.

He was forever sucking polos; and he cleaned his teeth whenever he got in after work. The mintiness of his mouth was what I noticed; not the underlying sourness. But did he think I'd make a fuss about his smoking? Did he think I'd forbid it? Well, I would have been horrified, wouldn't I? He was right to suspect me, wasn't he?

Even so, I think, as I slice the bread for toast, Brenda knew. Brenda smelt him out.

Nathan knew that Jacob was not as entirely dedicated to my well-being as I was to his.

The mist burns away in half an hour, leaving a brilliant May morning and the nostalgic scent of broom on the air.

When I see the two shadowy figures through the stained glass, panic arrests me. They'll have spotted my movement through the pane. They know I'm there as I know they're there. The tall shadow reaches out an arm and rings again. There is a blur of voices.

'Hello, Jacob. Hello, Hazel,' I open to them softly. 'Please do come in. And who are these little ones?' I ask, crouching to them. 'And a dog,' I say to Lara and Fergus, the easier visitors, 'you've got a lovely spaniel, what's his name? Come through everyone, come through,' I bustle. 'I'm sure we've got some cake for you. Do you like cherry cake? And fizzy pop?'

May emits a yelp and then a high-pitched scream when she recognises Jacob. She bursts into tears. Then she collects herself together to perform one of the most impressive theatrical turns of her life, in which he is welcomed back as the prodigal son but told not to expect anything in the way of fatted calf, to which she fervently objects on the grounds of veal-crates.

Yesterday we broke to her the news that Jacob had been found safe and well, and that he would be coming to see us with his . . . we groped for the right phrase: 'close friend' who has two children already, a boy and a girl, and who is expecting another baby. Gently I ended, 'Mum, it's . . . Jacob's . . . baby.'

I wonder sometimes if we don't underestimate May's shrewdness and toughness of mind. She measured up to the shock, if it was a shock, which surely it must have been, with animation.

'Am I to understand,' she broke in, 'that these other two are also of Jacob's begetting?'

'Oh no,' I wobbled and wavered on, softening all the details in the telling. 'This lady has led a very sad life and so naturally Jacob wants to take care of her . . . and it seems to me . . . tell me what you feel, I want to know . . . that we could welcome them all as part of our family. I know it's unconventional but why should that matter to us? If we know it's right? So what do you think?'

'About?'

'The baby and so forth.'

'That we should foster it?'

'Well, no, I didn't mean that, but kind-of become an extended family . . . to embrace them as part of us . . .'

'You're the boss, aren't you? You tell me.'

'Mum, hello, how are you?' Jacob, patchily red-faced, takes her hand and briefly pecks her on the cheek. 'This is my . . . Hazel. And these are her children, Lara and Fergus. And their dog, Laser.'

'Hi,' says Hazel.

Her hair is so pale it is almost white: honey-blonde, baby-blonde, and falls quite straight to her shoulders, where it tips and sways whenever she moves her head. The hair is really beautiful. I can imagine him aroused to wanting to touch it, to feel the cool pour of its silky fineness. In her embarrassment, she keeps looping soft strands of the hair behind one ear, from which it soon slides away.

She bites her lips and looks anywhere but in my eyes. My glance slides appraisingly to her figure and clothes, with many small pangs.

The way I perceive her transmits a shock through my body because it is charged with sexuality. I see her as I imagine Jacob first saw her – blonde and breasty, quite small, with a nervous hint of waif, skilfully made up so as to appear almost natural; only the eyes (which are pale blue and rather staring) surrounded by mascara, dominating the face. She wears a full T-shirt over white leggings. The pregnancy, which can't be more than five months developed, just shows as a fulness of flesh beneath the T-shirt.

'You are welcome,' says May in a courtly manner. 'I gather you are joining the family?'

The bale with which she extends this welcome is inexpressible.

'I'm sorry we didn't come and see you before,' Jacob says in a stammering dash, to cover the watery ferocity of his mother's pale glare. 'We had . . . a lot to sort out. I'm sorry you were worried.'

'You always were a difficult boy. We had the police, you know: they released a constable from his important duties in the Shrewsbury Male Voice Choir, specially to look for you. What do you have to say about that?'

All the while, May stares as if hypnotised at Hazel's white leggings.

'I'm really sorry, Mrs Copplestone,' Hazel ventures, tentatively.

'I bet. What do you call those . . . funny little hose you're wearing? Did she forget to change out of her pyjamas this morning? Or is she on her way to yoga?'

'Of course not, Mum,' I leap in, to quash further discussion of Hazel's legs. 'What about a nice cup of coffee and a bourbon biscuit? And the little ones can have something nice from the cake tin. I'm sure we've got something yummy in there,' I assure them. 'Jacob, you stay in here and keep Mum company and Hazel and I will go and sort out eats and drinks.'

I'm sounding so hearty; I must try to calm down my hammering pulse and stop acting like a parody of the Women's Institute. Hazel slides silently in behind me. Her children's hands rifle the biscuit tin and they shriek for cake. The spaniel patters round the alien kitchen sniffing. It pokes the cold curiosity of its nose up my skirt and snuffles. I bat the animal away.

'I'm so glad you felt you could come,' I say brightly, cradling my mug of hot coffee on the table between my leaning arms. 'I love Jacob – and because I love him so much and have done for so many years, I was glad of the opportunity to assure you that I care about you too – because anyone he cares about, I care about too.'

Flushing, she murmurs that it is nice of me.

'Not really. I admit it has been a shock.'

Head down, she seems to be humming to herself, studying the patterns on the ecological mug. I'm not getting it right. How can I get it right? There's so little time; it's like an exam, no leisure for cool reflection: just this pressure to scrape together the acceptable words that will bring success within reach.

It flashes on me to wonder what I would feel in this woman's situation.

Guilt, presumably; determination to keep my winnings at all costs; fear? alarm? But I could never be in her place: if God's prohibitions had not ensured that, my square jaw and squat figure would have done so. And the fact that I had my heart's desire in Jacob.

Her children racket around the garden, playing hide-and-seek on the terraces. Lara, who has run smack into the railings at the bottom, spots Jacob's boat on its moorings. Both pelt back up the garden: 'Look down

119

there! We've found a boat! A real one. Can we go out on that? Can we? Can we go now?'

'One day,' I promise, beaming. 'Soon. When you come again. Jacob will get the rowing boat ship-shape for you and we can all go for a trip up the river together. Won't that be lovely?'

'Count me out,' says their mother. 'I feel sick enough already.'

'Poor you,' I sympathise, dispensing further cake to her offspring. 'Has it been a bad pregnancy?'

'A bit sick. Under the weather.'

'But shouldn't that go off soon?'

She shrugs. 'Probably. It didn't last time.'

'*Is* it worse in the mornings? My sister Ellen said she was sick all day long with both of hers. Then she suddenly became well, and euphoric.'

'It depends.'

She is listening out for Jacob. As she restlessly peers through the adjoining door, the wheat-pale, silken hair swings to and fro; her whole attitude says, when can we get away from all this?

'In Bengal' and Bombay . . .', May is booming to Jacob. She soliloquises on the virtues of family life in the subcontinent of India, where after all their labours are done (and her life has been hard-working, she can tell him), old widows are honoured and esteemed by sons and not left to rot in shop-doorways with all their possessions in a supermarket trolley.

'I'm sorry, Mum,' he manages to get in. 'I'll often come to see you from now on.'

Hazel and I both watch. Doubly framed in two door-ways, Jacob leans forward, forearms on knees, to May who expresses indignant consciousness of affront to herself by leaning away from her son. The tug of filial loyalty Jacob genuinely feels towards May is visible in the way he reaches out and awkwardly pats his mother's black sleeve. But I see now, though it has never registered before, that what he feels for her has never qualified as affection, after his slapped and rebuked childhood.

Hazel gives a yawn. Her teeth are perfect. Mine are full of metal fillings.

'Are you tired?' I ask solicitously.

'I am, a bit.' She folds her arms flat on the table and props her breasts on them, almost as if she unconsciously displayed the attractions that had had the power to call my husband from my side. Again I see her sexually: she pulls my eyes and imagination into trespass. I colour up. It hurts to see how lovely her breasts are. I look away towards ripples of light cast by the rocking boughs of the beech on the wall.

'I do hope we'll be able to be friends, it would mean a lot to me, Hazel.'

'Excuse me . . .' she says diffidently, 'but why are you doing all this exactly?'

'Doing what?'

'Trying to . . . take me and the kids on? Is it being . . . Christian and so on – you feel it's your . . . duty?' She loops another tendril of baby-blonde hair back over her ear and I watch it slide. Her skin is so fair as to seem transparent: a flush comes and goes with the waves of discomfort. 'Excuse my asking.'

My skin must seem like hide, my bulk lumpen, beside that sylph.

Jacob kisses those full, pale lips; he lies beside, astride, above, beneath that girlish body.

'I suppose,' I hear myself plodding on, according to the map I'd previously sketched, 'now that the . . . first shock is over, I want to build again – a new life for myself and all of us – and if that can be on a basis of good feeling and family love, the better for me and everyone.'

'Gosh,' is all she says, sagging back.

Is that all she can say?

'Does it all seem so . . . ridiculous to you?'

'No – it's all very generous and so on, but . . . oh, I don't know, it doesn't seem quite real somehow . . . people just don't live in the world you're imagining. Sorry if that's . . .' She tails off.

'Maybe we've lived in different worlds?'

'Yes.'

'And yours has had too much pain. And mine has had surplus happiness. And we've just swapped places. There's some justice in that.'

She stares; takes a deep breath; has perhaps divined that I am mad. 'Well, okay, if you think so. But wouldn't a clean break be the best thing?'

'No. Honestly. And besides, we've got the Oldies to consider. You haven't met Brenda yet, have you? She's lovely. And the baby will be May's grandchild, after all.'

Hazel's face is eloquent on that aspect of her child's genetic inheritance.

'Was she always like that? Or is it Alzheimer's?'

'With May,' I explain, 'I think she's just broken out – sort-of too late to do anything creative with her brains. I don't think she's ill at all. She had a really strict Calvinist upbringing, you see, and had her energies bottled up . . . and old age gave her a chance to escape. So she's broken out.'

'Like Jake,' comments Hazel, and for the first time in our meeting she seems kindled by what I have to say. I startle and shudder at the nickname. My Jacob is her Jake. I go silent. For some reason that renaming acutely needles. 'Why don't you just put them all in a home if you want a life of your own?' she enquires off-handedly. 'After all, they're not your relatives.'

This summary disposal of our kin somehow exhausts my reserves. I mutter, 'That's . . . not how I see it.'

'You're so motherly,' she observes. 'That's what Jacob says. You want to smoth- . . . I mean, mother people and people want to be mothered by you. Pity you couldn't have children of your own,' she ends matter-of-factly.

May says, in a loud voice, 'He's to report once a week, Dee Dee, make a note of it in the log. He's on parole.'

Jacob comes in, rubbing his eyes with the palms of both hands.

'Yes, Mother,' I say in a humouring voice. For a moment all three of us are one, exchanging mirroring looks of complicity. 'Go and put the tele on for her, Jacob, would you,' I murmur. 'It'll take her mind off the prison system.'

When he returns he hovers between two chairs, one next to Hazel and the other next to me. Impossible to look him in the face; my eyes focus on the lapel of his jacket and part of his shoulder.

'What we are worrying about, Jessie,' he says to me, 'is the baby . . . you see, we don't want him to be born outside marriage – and we wonder if you'd consider giving us what's called a "quickie divorce", meaning that you cite me for adultery – and if we get going fairly sharply, Hazel and I could be married by the time of the birth. What do you think?'

They both turn hopeful, expectant faces upon me as if the request were the most natural thing in the world for me to grant. I take the scorch of their double gaze full in the eyes.

'That's something . . . we'd need to talk about

privately, Jacob,' I pant. 'And I'd have to think about it deeply before I could give you any answer. Please understand, for me marriage is sacramental – it is for life – the vows . . . are real . . . and binding.'

He blenches; she sneaks a rueful look at him as I struggle enmeshed in the net of principle, desire and stratagem. Catching the look at once angers and dismays me. I temporise: 'Surely illegitimacy doesn't carry the same stigma nowadays?'

'Well, no,' says Jacob. 'But I felt you'd agree that . . . he shouldn't be born without my name. Goodness – is that the time? Please do think about it, Jessie.'

'Don't go,' I murmur faintly. 'It would be so nice for us to have a meal together.'

'Sorry, Jess. Another time,' mumbles Jacob. Hazel ushers her hectic children out into the hall ahead of her. The three of them disappear, leaving Jacob half in, half out of the morning-room door.

'But it's so important – to eat together,' I burst out. 'Please don't go. Please would you stay?'

'As I say – another time. You'll be all right, Jess. Really you will,' he assures, implores.

'Jake,' comes a voice from the hall. 'Lara feels sick – she's had too much cake.'

'Well, if you really can't stay, Jacob, perhaps we could agree a time to discuss the . . . matter you mentioned.'

I follow in the wake of their stampede to the front door, all valedictions and Godspeeds.

Haughmond is more beautiful at this time of year than one can ever remember from one year to the next. Acres of curving green meadow, with sheep, nothing but sheep, a hubbub of bleating for miles around, and the sough and seethe of wind in the trees. Leaving Cathy's car in the Abbey park, I take the wind in my face and all my hair flies up on end. The lightscape over the far hills takes away my breath as I cross the road to Haughmond Hill; climb the stile; move into cover.

Almost at once the beeches cover me with canopies, trailing their skirts in natural arches over the path so that I move through a tunnel of greenness, as the traffic roar recedes. Waves of wind break on the thrashing outer trees that fence the hush within.

I tread this tunnel through a thousand aspects of green, light dappling through great bodies of oak and beech. Shadows slant sidelong from the avenue of ancient trunks; the remnant of an original mantle of trees that covered most of our world before we hacked it back. An inner forest of ferns on the hillside unfurls from embryo. Commotion of rustlings; hauntings of birdsong; glitterings of sifted light.

Take my car, said Cathy, *get out into the country – get away from it all.*

They were all down with stinking colds, she said; and Joe seemed to have ear-ache.

She insisted on having an account of Jacob's visit, and *Oh God*, she burst out in her hoarse voice, *I hate that man, how I hate that man.*

Oh Cathy, don't say that.

But I do, I hate him – I'd like to . . . I'd like to . . . castrate the bastard and . . . strangle him . . . and . . . how dare he? How dare he, the selfish bastard?

Cathy! I half-laughed, through shock and a complex relief that I could hear the words I hardly dared think, said for me. Complex, though, because it is unnerving to hear my Jacob, still part of me, condemned as unworthy; needing him, longing for him back.

I'm sorry, I can't help it – I think the way he's behaved to you is despicable.

But Cathy, I love him, you see – he's my husband.

She was quiet for a moment, a child wailing in the background. She blew her nose.

I'm sorry but it's just so awful to see you suffer. Look, I don't want you to catch this bug but . . . take my car, get out into the country . . .

It was an inspiration. I climb now to Queen Eleanor's Bower where my eye sweeps the plain and my face scalds in the blast. The muscles of my thighs burn, and I'm sweating and panting. My mind has turned inside-out, emptying all but a sifting of pain, which seems to stream away on the wind, leaving me in an amnesiac trance. Stumbling back the way I came, I crunch an apple. I scarcely think of Jacob, Hazel, May, Brenda, Nella, anyone.

Later, wearier, I skirt the Quarry with its bellowing machines and wander the conifer plantation amongst swaying pillars of pines and birch saplings, sent into shimmering hysteria by every gust. A pine startles me by creaking. Several others have fallen on to it and in every wind they all creak uneasily against the load-bearer. Resin fumes in the air. Subsiding on a fallen log, I call to mind the hermit's effigy in Shrewsbury Abbey. That barren stone; that life of luxurious immunity to others' needs. I feel the potency of such a dream of apartness: aloneness which up till now has always spelt dread.

Whole streets in Belle Vue are named after his selfish sequestration: Hermitage. What streets are named after us? Unpaid Labour Street. Drudge Avenue.

And, Cathy, I said, *to top it all, May had a fall after he and Hazel left, fractured a thigh and she's been taken in to the Royal Orthopaedic.*

There was another pause, and then Cathy, the gentle, the mild and clement, the excessively charitable, said, *Good. Give you a rest.*

May was so strange after they went. I recognise that with hindsight; at the time I was glazed, paralysed. I sat with my head against the wall. My shoulders shuddered in throes of shock, and my vision was composed of cruising dots; atoms travelling randomly, disintegrating and reforming into temporary pictures of my hand with the wedding ring; the lamp; a coating of dust on the piano; and May.

May whose face seemed to be working inscrutably. If I piece the perceptions together in retrospect, I see her turn her neck, open her mouth, close it again, look at me searchingly and sharply swivel away. I dwell on that searching look. If I did not know May ... if another person had fixed me with that naked look ... I would have interpreted it as compassion.

She hoisted herself up from the chair, took a step towards me, caught her foot in the mat and fell sprawling.

Over the quilt of shed needles I make my way back to Cathy's car, having met not a soul all morning, my eyes rinsed and salved by the greenness and the light.

CHAPTER 9

On the chapel forecourt, as I arrive for the service, streaming with cold, hands flutter on my arm; kind mouths tender healing phrases: everyday words, whose comfort is in the manner rather than the substance of what is said. Sensitive souls encompass me in the larger web of belonging that binds me in to a community with Christ at its centre. But my portion of the web is frail and frayed. Although I home to the company of these brothers and sisters I've known since childhood, I am detached at nearly every point from their certainties.

Beneath the over-arching willows on the river path I paused to pray, 'Dear Jesus, point me the way.'

But the eye of my faith was bleary, bloodshot. And if Jesus didn't audibly respond to my prayer, isn't that because I've never needed Jesus the way I needed Jacob: what can I expect of my second-best friend?

'How are you, Jessie?'

'How are you managing, dear?'

'We've been thinking of you.'

'Praying for you.'

I answer that I'm a bit groggy with a cold: don't get too close. I don't want them to catch it. Hardly anyone backs off.

The visiting speaker from Llangollen presents a colourful and complacent account of the work of the mission in Malawi. The flock is braced by this and fortified by its sense of belonging to a community of souls reaching far beyond Shropshire's margins; in which Severn-dwellers can furnish from their undeserved plenty means of irrigation to drought-struck Africans.

PEACE GRACE CHARITY FAITH HOPE LIGHT: I lift my eyes to the heights of this golden lettering but the coughing fit I've been struggling to restrain explodes; my neighbours politely feigning not to notice. A resonant cry of 'Praise the Lord!' challenges the potency of my virus; and a bout of 'Hallelujah!'s drowns it out. Mr Troubridge, with a wink, passes me two sweets from a packet of Tunes.

We emerge into a steady drizzle and muffled peals of bells.

Peter is here: 'My dear dear Jess – how are you? I'd heard you'd not been well.'

'Just a bad cold. But it put me out of action. Did you know May's been admitted to hospital?'

He has heard. Says he hopes it's not uncharitable of him to say so because of the sincere concern he feels for dear May, but he imagines it at least gives me a bit of respite?

The quiet of the household is astonishing. Sometimes it registers as an eerie silence broken only by the shouting of the coxes as the boats shoot past the window; at others, as a kind of ebb of desire as I drowse, mind furred and fogged by catarrh. May expects to be in there for at least a month. Appears in her element, the centre of a dynamic drama in which the whole hospital revolves around her X-rays, her blood-tests and the possibility of her manifesting some fabulously rare polysyllabic disease. She instructs the doctors on the abstruser aspects of their science and amuses the nurses with her condemnation of the consultants' wealth; her Maoist conviction that they would benefit from a spell as navvies. Me she has ordered off until I am germ-free, arguing that there are enough germs already in the hospital without importing foreign strains.

Once I would have denied, both to myself and others, the relief her absence brings. Now I freely confess, 'Yes, Peter, it does mean I can get some rest. And of course Brenda is no trouble.'

She is becoming bed-bound. But she lies there quietly and doesn't complain. One of her ex-pupils is in town between jobs and has been keeping her company in the afternoons. I'm all but redundant.

'I intend visiting dear May this evening,' says Peter. 'Does she like grapes?'

'Oh yes. Don't be surprised if she doesn't take much notice of you. She's kept pretty busy reorganising the NHS.'

Illness has given me permission to live for myself, taking time off from others' needs. Illness is my morphine, insulating my nervous system against penetration by their pain. I fell back into its lap and lay there with my conscience switched off. Jacob and Hazel seemed to withdraw to a hazy periphery.

'I'm ill in bed. Your mum's in hospital,' I croaked to Jacob when he rang.

'Oh lord, Jess. Poor you. When are you likely to be well enough to talk?'

'I'll let you know, love.'

'It's just that . . . I'm sorry you're poorly but we need to get moving fairly fast. We've seen our solicitor . . .'

'Not yet, Jacob. Sorry. No fit state.'

'Well, let me know when you're up to it. Can I get you any shopping in?' he asked as an afterthought.

Putting down the receiver, I turned over with a

flouncing shrug and fell fast asleep, in the arms of my blessed virus.

I didn't want to recover. Wanted to lie there indefinitely, cocooned in Nathan's single bed (I've moved out of our bedroom), groggily gazing at the portable TV, hot weak tea slipping down my raging throat. The weight of quiet insulated me, a counterpane of deafness.

This morning when I woke, I could no longer pretend to myself that I was still legitimately out of action; with a healthy appetite I ate toast and marmalade with the window open, breathing in the sabbath freshness, and thought I'd come to church.

Though in spiritual terms it was no success, it has brought me out into the company of people I care about; and I look forward to the oceans of quiet that await me at home.

But Jacob is on the phone.

'How are you? . . . Oh *good*, what a relief. Can I come round?'

'Oh Jacob, do you mind not coming . . . quite so soon; I just don't feel quite ready to talk to you yet.'

' . . . Why not?'

'I just feel that I do need a bit of space.'

'But Jessie . . . dear . . . there's so little time left, and I know you want to do what's best for all of us. After all, you said to Hazel that you'd like to take her under your wing . . . and so we thought you . . .'

'I'm sure I never said anything so priggish as that about . . . taking her under my wing – I'm sure I can't have said that.'

'Well, no, but words to that effect. It sounds like you . . . like your kind, compassionate way of speaking.' The coaxing voice strokes me in the privacy of my inner ear without shame. I realise he needs me: not as I want to be needed, but to provide something he and she cannot afford to be without and only I can supply.

'I *do* want to do what's right for all of us but I'm just not sure what it is yet.'

'I don't want to push you, Jess, but things are quite tough at this end, especially for Hazel, and if I could just pop round . . .'

'Sorry, Jacob, but I . . .'

' . . . pop round, Jessie, and have a little chat. I know how much you care about us all and it's meant a lot to me, so, even if you don't feel quite A1, do you mind if I come?'

I take a deep breath. The brittle urgency in his voice is a new thing for him. Always a gently spoken man, he never barged through barriers against people's will. It was his habit to glide round obstacles, or to back off, seldom to meet them head-on. *What's the point of getting people's backs up?* he'd quietly enquire. Now he is set in his determination to have his desire. His desire is sharp. 'Well, love,' I reply, 'Actually – sorry – but, don't come. It's not the right time. Okay?'

'Not really, Jessie. Time is what we just don't have.'

He's raiding the peace my virus left in its wake. He mars the view of the flow of the river from my window; a spell of time to myself, for reflection, as the trees on the other bank reflect on their challenged images on water, breaking and repairing, rootfast and flowing. The rage in me explodes in a sudden sulk, like a child's, and I burst out hoarsely, 'Look, Jacob, you're spoiling my day!'

I don't say you've spoilt my life.

I only bear witness to the clouding of the present light; the green day of respite I've stolen for myself.

When he puts down the phone, there's a ringing echo in my ears and the view from the window is not only drab but full of anxious premonition. The boughs of the limes flurry in directionless anarchy and pointless blackbirds flit from tree to tree. I blow my nose resoundingly. Why should he be allowed to spoil my day?

I put on a tape of Dvorak's American quartet; and, looking out of the window, find that the boughs are rocking to the music in a wild fandango.

I turn the music up higher.

And the turbulence turns to dance.

But when I open the door, he's there poised on the top step, wearing a new suede jacket, with his doorkey out.

'I just have to talk to you,' he says. 'Please. Sorry.'

Pushes through. Sits down in his old leather chair. I ache, melt, with longing, through my rage.

Wants me to promise a divorce. Instant. Seems to want it tomorrow morning at the latest. Looks hunted, trapped.

'This is not you talking, Jacob.'

He doesn't want to be unkind, but sometimes it's kindest in the long run to state things straight out.

My back stiffens by the moment. Go on like that and I will hate you. In hate is hope. The violins rampage in a tempest of ecstasy as Dvorak celebrates his homeland in the New World. I snap the tape off. The music is nothing to do with him. It's mine. Hope in that too.

We do need to think about the baby, he urges me. The baby's good has to be paramount.

I walk to the piano and return with the photograph of Nella fishing at the Canal; grin of gap-toothed cocky jubilation at her silver catch, tangled mass of hair under Jacob's canvas cap, galoshes, skirt tucked into her knickers. I hand the picture down to Jacob.

'Do you ever think of Nella, Jacob, nowadays?'

'What has she got to do with it?' He hands back the photo without looking at it.

How strange that Nella's eyes were so like Jacob's. People would remark upon the resemblance.

Nella and me at the buttercup-meadow behind the Weir, offering fresh, sweet grass to the mare and her foal over the fence; Nella squealing at the tickling rasp of the mare's tongue on her palm, her whole excitable body in a shiver. Eyes so like Jacob's.

'About the divorce...'

He pounds that word, *divorce*, a word that splits me wide apart, a word that casually blasphemes all that I have valued and discounts all I've tried to be.

'I can't – at present – countenance such a step, Jacob.'

I never imagined he could be so brutal in pursuit of his ends.

'Okay then, but you'd better make up your mind soon.'

His rust-coloured suede jacket – new? an off-the-peg Jacob? – emits an animal scent, a male scent somehow, at once troubling and arousing to me.

What did it cost?

Whose money?

'Because,' he goes on, 'if you won't divorce me, I'll have to divorce you.'

'What? – On what possible grounds?'

'Unreasonable behaviour is sufficient grounds.'

'But what unreasonable behaviour?' I burst out. 'What have I ever done in my life to hurt you?'

He won't specify; seems abashed. Well, he's sure it won't come to that. He looks at my livid face with hangdog regret.

'Sorry. It's all the strain,' he explains.

He'll just take one or two things with him while he's here.

Jacob produces from the suede coat pocket a long list of items, in two styles of handwriting, his and hers.

Boxes of clothes, books, tools, are collected and marched out to the van.

He'll be in touch.

That bastard, said Cathy. *God, I hate him*, she said.

I'm due to visit his mother this evening. I passionately resent the prospect, I absolutely don't want her back.

Brenda and her geographer friend are practising Zen meditation exercises together, Averil being an amateur of alternative therapies who has tried out all four local Natural Health Centres and picked up tips from a yogi in Harlescott. They have been listening to me barging and stumbling round the house, hardly knowing what I was doing, but needing to keep on the move, as if I could physically remove myself from the memory of Jacob's brutal ditching of me in favour of Hazel and their coming baby. That baby will have his eyes. The beautiful eyes hunt me, haunt me, from room to room.

'What you feel,' says Averil, 'is legitimate rage. You must let your rage out.'

It's therapeutic, she explains, to learn to swear and punch. 'You need a surrogate.'

'Pardon?'

'A surrogate for the person who has injured you. Look here, I'll build you one and then you lambast him.'

'That doesn't sound like Buddhism.'

'No, it isn't – it's pick'n'mix.'

She begins to set up an imaginary Jacob in the form of a pile of cushions in his chair, inviting me to vent all my rage on the cushion-Jacob. Kick him, punch him, tear him limb from spongy limb and hurl his mutilated anatomy into the four quarters of the room, having first taken care (says Averil) to remove breakable objects such as the lamp-standard and ornaments. Anger makes you ill if you store it; also it breeds like tumours and indeed it can cause cancer.

'Get her to express her anger in a safe context,' Averil advises Brenda, when I decline, fairly politely, to punch the cushions: 'teach her martial arts and perhaps karate.'

'The poor woman has no sense of humour,' says Brenda apologetically after Averil has gone. 'She has been swept perhaps a little too far along in the direction of holistic thises and thats. She is young, only fifty-two, and hence liable to enthusiasms.'

However, before she left, Averil had Brenda and me doing yoga exercises according to our different capabilities, hers being chiefly limited to the movements of the wrists and elbows.

Now – BREATHE.

Pretending to be a variety of surprising animals, from monkeys and rabbits to cobras fitted in perfectly with my manic state of mind.

'I like your lion very much, Jessie,' our guru complimented me. 'Your lion definitely has a future. Yes, a *very* nasty face indeed. And now, girls, we shall finish with the asana which is commonly referred to by the Yogis as The Peace of Unity.'

Later, still roving the house, pulsing with pain and rage, I caught sight of the surrogate Jacob still dominating the couch. Obscenely plump he sat, and pink, and velvet. I slammed a blow into his complacent guts.

'How – dare – you?' I shrieked.

His oafish head flew off. Picking it up, I rammed it back on to his body and pounded it with both fists, hollering and screaming.

'Is everything all right, dear?' called Brenda's querulous voice.

'I'm just – thrashing – that fucking fucking blasted bastard ...'

'Oh, *good*, dear – keep it up.'

I whacked his sordid, ruthless head against the wall, three times, four times, so that the dust flew out of the cushion and the glasses on the dresser jingled. I flung his remains around the room. I stamped his private parts into pulp.

'How are you getting on, dear?' called Brenda from the morning room. 'I'm sure it's therapeutic but don't do yourself any damage.'

Sweating, crying with laughter, I collapsed into the vacated couch.

'Okay,' I reassured her. 'I've done for now. You shit, you wanker,' I added as a postscript, diminuendo. 'You ungrateful prick.'

Aghast, incredulous, the old me looked on at the new me's berserk performance, wondering where in Heaven's name I had picked up such language. What am I becoming? Of course May curses like a trooper; perhaps I've gleaned my obscenities from her.

On impulse I clamber down the rusted ladder to Jacob's old boat. It laps where for years it's been rotting on its moorings, tether green with algae, slack or taut, nudging the wall, sidling outwards. My clumsy embarkation pitches it from side to side until I can negotiate my weight into the centre and sit ponderously down; cast off the line.

A minor haunting. I am sitting where Jacob sat, my hands on the oars he commanded, when he took me and Nella out for Saturday jaunts. And always she'd insist on being captain, squeezed up against him and pulling like mad, her oar sloshing, scooping, skimming, delving deep troughs in the water: Jacob compensating for her zealous ineptitude, throwing me the slightest wrinkling grin with his eyes. Such vitality, I've never seen before or since, as Nella's. As for me, I never aspired to row but lolled in the prow, taking time off, dabbling my fingers in the cool, musing on the slide and swell of dappled water's green and black.

Why don't you try Mama? Go on, it's great.

So late in the day, I make a stab at it. The boat drifts downstream, wobbling on the enigma of the waters while I fight to slot the oars into their supports and find myself back-to-front sailing down the wrong side of the river in the wrong direction. As I manoeuvre to turn, the boat lurches and the oars swivel in their sockets.

With panting labour, I turn the boat upstream and begin to pull. Crash into willow; push out. The trick is to learn to do the opposite to what you're accustomed to doing. Travel backwards. The trick is ... if you want to go right, Jessie, pull left ... yes.

The muscles of my arms and thighs burn as I pull round the loop of the river towards the Quarry; my sore bottom slides to and fro on the seat. Out of condition. Sweating. Right hand stronger than left so I travel obliquely out to the centre and correct myself in a series of crazy zigzags, to laughter from a passing coxless eight. But I seem to catch the ghost of Jacob's long-ago instruction to Nella, *Don't bury your oar, love, just dip it in so it's covered, that's the way.* I follow the directive. But now my whimsical oars just skitter on the surface, with a plume of foam. *Cover your oar, that's it, and lift it clear, don't drag, that's the ticket.*

I'm fat and unfit but I'm getting the hang. Red, panting rage jerks the boat forward, rounding the bend until Chad's is well in view. Rush forward; rest; rush forward; rest. The rhythm mesmerises me; I move past premature exhaustion into the premonition of long-term strength as I haul along, round, opposite the school, under the Porthill suspension bridge, beneath the Boathouse Inn where couples are out on the balcony, and a purring hum of talk and convivial laughter reaches me.

Beyond the Welsh Bridge, I cursorily admire the blisters on my palms; turn for home and steer downstream with better confidence, pluming myself, on the level of the swans. All in, I tie the boat, lug myself up the ladder and cross the garden, in jelly-kneed weakness.

Before the euphoria can wear off, I have written the letter Jacob has been soliciting. If you really want a divorce, I write, I will co-operate.

I'll see my solicitor this week about details of the settlement.

I shall almost certainly need to return to work, or be retrained. Please let me know in due course what arrangements you intend to make about the care of your mother.

I don't put a stamp on the letter; I may decide not to send it, after all, and I wouldn't want to waste the postage on carriage for a bomb my conscience doesn't permit me to drop.

I don't want May here.

I don't want to be a carer.

I can't stand the thought of having my life taken out of my own hands again.

If I'm to lose Jacob, there should be some compensation.

> These are evil thoughts.
> May is still my responsibility.
> Women are natural carers.
> Everyone will blame me.

No one will blame me. They will say, *How did she cope with that for so many years?*. They will say, *Poor Jess*.

I did my best. Now it's his turn.

   May's poor face will turn to me in raging panic.

   May will die in some dreadful home and I'll always blame myself. I'll never sleep a wink after that.

I want a life.

Of my own.

I want my life back.

I have needs.

Why do my needs not count, never count, never have counted?

   You will hate yourself forever after if you pack her off.

   Your whole life has been built on selflessness.

   You will have let your parents down and your God.

   You won't be Jessie after that.

   It is the unforgivable sin. You'll never atone.

What about Jacob's responsibilities?

She's his mother, not mine.

Let him cope.

Why should Jacob go whistling off into a new bed – leaving me only a smoky, decaying jersey to cuddle? Liar, forsaker, fornicator.

   Jacob's a man.

   Higgamus hoggamus.

   Men have more rights.

   People will say, Jessie Copplestone can't be so saintly after all, she's ditched her mother-in-law, she must have driven him to leave her.

   And, Jessie, you need to belong, to be embraced, and validated, you can't survive alone.

Just because you can row a boat a mile ... so what?

I matter.

I should be happy.

I hate Jacob, I loathe Hazel.

I'm being exploited, I've been used for years.

But, Jessie, the baby ...

The conclusive baby ...

Nella, Nella, my Nella

You are despicable to even think of hitting back at Jacob through hurting another human being.

Ruefully, I stare at the letterbox into which I've just posted a version of the letter. The moment it was in there, I knew it was a mistake. I could always wait for the postman to come and collect the mail and ask for it back.

But I think there's a regulation that prohibits them from doing that.

I'll go home and write another one telling him not to take any notice of that other letter, and he'll get them both by the same post. I could write 'Open this first' on the new one, and instruct him to tear up the second.

But I do neither. I drowse off in front of the gasfire and awaken with a sense of inertia.

May is on cracking form, holding forth with such fluency that I am scarcely called upon to contribute more than single phrases. I huddle beside the bed in a plastic seat not built for the human back, sunk into a condition of blank, exhausted dismay.

May praises the way of life in here; plenty of bustle, white-coats coming and going, everybody listing their symptoms like strings of sausages. She's told hers to seven young junior doctors and the Big White Chief himself, and dozens of jolly nurses sticking therm-ometers in her armpit. Hair-line crack in thigh-bone has a Latin name, she wrote it down, fish it out, Dee Dee, no not in there – there, over there – fit for an Emperor to have engraved on his tomb. She's made a bosom friend of Mrs Jenkins on her right, a real talker she is and given to wandering off the point but May sets her straight; on her left a lady from Bengal originally, very quiet and decent sort.

'Your nose is red. Have your germs gone? Because if not you must scat.'

The temptation to report sick is piercing. Instead I ask, 'How are you, Mother?'

'Worse, much worse.' She shakes her head, majestic in tribulation.

'Oh dear. How are they treating you?'

They're working on her. She's a very complicated case. Yesterday, she had a bodyscan. She was inserted into a giant magnet. They said she was very brave. They said they'd never seen anything like it.

'I'm sure you were.'

Mind you, the cooking is not what it might be. Cold toad in the hole. Eggs salmonella. Not that she's grum-bling: it must be remembered that Dee Dee runs a far smaller establishment, and has the time and energy to be able to serve up home-cooked hot meals, whereas here they're catering for hundreds at a time.

She then prods me with one forefinger and accuses me of thinking that this is a hospital ward.

'Well, it is, isn't it, May?'

She scoffs. 'Fat lot you know. It's really a college, it's a sort of sub-medical college, an ancillary college which is attached to the main Medical School – and I'm going to be the oldest medical student. What about that then? Bit of a problem though ... come a bit nearer, I don't want to shout . . . One of the doctors (I won't tell you his name in case we're being bugged) wants to have SEX with me.'

'Oh, I'm sure you're mistaken, May.'

'Such a prude, you always were, you know. Don't fidget, Dee Dee. I don't want people to think I'm boring you. And stop wriggling. Of course, *he* hasn't been to see me. Oh no. While I think about it, Dee Dee, there's a load of washing piled up waiting for you, which would you please take home, yes it's in there . . . all that . . . yes, and that pink bedshawl . . . and Mrs Jenkins needs some laundry doing too, my friend Mrs Jenkins, yes that lady there, Mrs Delyth Jenkins, she's got quite a lot of laundry and no nearest and dearest to attend to it for her, so would you take that too please, I don't think it would be too much trouble for you, because I know how much you love keeping people clean.'

I rise mutely, and begin to stuff their washing into two Safeway bags.

'What are you looking huffy for, miss?' she asks sharply.

'Nothing, I'm not huffy, I'm just rather tired.'

'Tired! *You're* tired!' she hoots.

'Yes – I'm tired. Anything else, May?'

'Not as of the present moment, no. This lady on the other side, she's from Bengal, she's a Hindu, we have all religions at our academy, we're ecumenical, this lady has an idol of the god Shiva on her cabinet. You think it's wonderful if some Methodists and the Welshmen from Eglwys y Taberncl all manage to get together in your ruddy Baptist Church and sing your hymns to the tambourine . . . I tell you, you know nothing about internationalism. Out here, we're International House, we are.'

'Oh,' I say, hot and sick. 'That's interesting.'

'Let me introduce you to people now.'

She does so, in virtuoso style, and at length.

'She's very quiet, isn't she, your daughter-in-law?' observes Mrs Jenkins as I edge towards leaving.

'Well, she's the homely type,' she explains to Mrs Jenkins. 'Likes to stay in and bake. Her ambition was a higher form of chiropody but she never achieved it, poor thing.'

'Now me, I like gossip. Give me a good gossip over a pot of tea any day.'

'Oh, and me. Hearing ill of my neighbour is my main hobby.'

Mrs Jenkins, who is not a plain-speaker, shoots May an unsettled look.

'But my daughter-in-law won't have it in the house,' May goes on.

'What?'

'Gossip. She's a puritan you see. Thinks God is listening in to your every word and monitoring it on the Internet.'

'Oh *duw*. How do you get on for conversation then, *bach*?'

I stand at the bottom of the bed, trying to slip away, but each time I take a step towards the door, May recalls me to receive a last succulent morsel of tattle.

Mrs Jenkins' next-door neighbour has transmitted entertaining snippets of a titillating nature concerning a sixty-four-year-old lady down their street who has taken a forty-eight-year-old lodger whose rent is paid in kind. A vegetarian apparently, but lascivious. Behind those net curtains it's nut cutlets followed by tumbling on the futon. The neighbour, a Mrs Price, listens through a glass to grunts and twangings, which confirm the sightings she has made whilst pegging clothes on her line.

What would you prefer, May has asked Mrs Jenkins: *a choice of ecstasy or respectability?*

She has been reading a magazine article about the female orgasm. She passed it across to Mrs Jenkins.

Oh you are a one, said Mrs Jenkins, but she was apparently deaf-mute for an hour afterwards, profoundly absorbed.

In the end, I simply depart, in the middle of one of her sentences, walk fast, then take to my heels down the corridor. I hurl my twin laundry burdens into the back of the cab, and whisper under my breath an incantation of curses.

Chapter 10

The theological problem of Mrs Jenkins' washing pre-occupies me. For whereas previously I'd have been only too happy to have put Mrs Jenkins' stuff round with May's, considering it my Christian and neighbourly duty, now I find myself resenting the imposition of this other old woman's washing on top of the existing old woman's washing.

I mean, why not set up as a charitable laundress and go round collecting the dirty garments of anyone who chooses to bestow them on me?

I stoop to bundle the contents of the two Safeways bags into the washing machine; lock the door; set the programme.

– What's all the fuss about? the old Jessie asks the new one. Trifling extra trouble involved for you and it helps an infirm old person out. What are you grumbling about?

Because I'm put upon, that's what. I'm just used as a beast of burden.

– But it's nothing. Look, the machine is doing it all for you anyway. And as Jesus says, For as much as you do it unto the least of these my children, you do it unto me.

Who did Jesus' washing, I'd like to know? Some poor

female unmentioned in the Gospel, no doubt – or a team of laundresses tagging along.

– Jessie!

Next time she grandly lands me with some thankless menial job, I'm going to say no. Mrs Jenkins can make her own arrangements.

– But Jessie, she has no one.

– That poor woman has no one.

My cornered spirit grinds against the conditions of its confinement. Rain tips down outside and the washing machine roars as it mingles May's nighties with Mrs Jenkins', without distinction of person.

I'm ashamed of myself: the depths to which I have already sunk and the fact that I am still falling. Settling on my beanbag chair in front of the roaring gasfire with a mug of coffee, I console myself with the prospect of yet another blissful night off from May's midnight furores. Sleep . . . the necessary sleep . . . starved of it for literally years, though invaded by nightmares of Jacob lost, is something that, now I've got it back, I'd kill to keep.

Sleep is the bottom line.

'How was she?' asks Brenda when I've recovered from my quarrel with myself enough to go in and chat with her.

'She got me to take her neighbour's washing as well as hers.'

'Oh honestly.'

'Well, apparently, this lady has no one to take care of her personal things, so it made sense. It's just . . . oh you know the way May has of laying down the law. The sister says the ward will keep her until she's fully mobile. Said she's as nice as ninepence.'

'Good gracious.'

'They're inclined to think there's no identifiable

disease, Brennie ... just the broken leg. They're going to get the physio in when the break has mended – I spoke to her, and she thinks there's nothing to stop May becoming fully mobile – "going out shopping and for walks in the park" – except ...'

'Except May.'

Far-away-eyed Brenda says she will not get up today if I don't mind. Averil will be visiting for an afternoon of self-healing by the incantation of astral rays.

'Of course,' she adds, to protect her scientific integrity, 'I don't believe in it literally – it's all moonshine – but the incantations are most soothing.'

'Omm?' I have heard them chanting 'Omm' beside a candle.

'No, dear. More a kind of sussuration. Conjures up frying bacon and reeds in a high wind.'

From the kitchen, whipping up an omelette, I overhear Brenda sussurating.

Two frail hands may be spied wafting in the air, in apparent sign of blessing.

I extract the mound of washing from the machine and sort it into Hers and Hers.

When the phone rings, it's Nathan.

'I've some news for you, Jessie. Rather good news.' He sounds nervous.

'What is it, love?'

'Well, I'm going to have a double room after all.'

'Oh, but Nathan ...'

'No, dear ... I'm going to share it, you see, with a lady. Well, when I've married her, of course. Not until such time.'

'Dearest ...'

'Yes, I know it's sudden,' he hurries on. 'But at our

age, you know, there's no time to be lost – really, every day that passes brings us nearer the Bourne.'

'The Born?'

'The Bourne Whence. You know. Whence No Traveller Returns. So we felt . . . Dorothy and I . . . that's my friend, Dorothy . . . who's a Friend, you see . . .'

'Nathan, I'm not following you at all, I'm afraid.'

'A Friend. A Quaker.'

'Oh. Right.'

'We both prayed singly and apart, to assess whether this was a Divine Leading – and we came to the same conclusion – that it must be . . . so why bother with preliminaries, courtship and so forth? Anyway, we're getting married three weeks on Wednesday, we have the first slot at the Registry Office, a lovely lady registrar will hear our vows, and then we shall have a half hour of celebratory silence at her brother's home, followed by a modest spread, nothing fancy, just a sandwich and a cup of tea . . . and may I hope, Jessie dear, that you will be a witness?'

'Of course – of course – and I'm so happy for you.'

'Now,' he goes on hoarsely. 'I don't want you to feel left out. I don't want you to feel that I . . . have ceased to feel . . . that you are the most precious, most loving, most tender being on earth. In fact I told Dorothy all about you when we saw you out rowing on the river. And she is longing to meet you on dry land. She says how glad she is that I've had someone like you in my life . . .'

Someone like you in my life. If only he knew.

As I drift from the phone to the window, I see my own shadowy image eddying towards myself. The person they still recognise as Jessie: the self-giver, the tender-hearted. I want her back, I want to merge back into her . . . and if I do, only Brenda will ever know how I have parted company with her under this stress.

I've no idea if it can be done. It seems like a conjuring trick.

Perhaps if I cannot be that person exactly (and not all of me wants to be her), there can be some new woman born of her, not utterly unrecognisable: less of an idealist, with fewer illusions, tougher.

– A modern Jess Copplestone, mocks an inner voice.

Well, and why not?

'Brennie, I'm going shopping. Anything you need?'

I'm stuck in the past, alongside all these fading folk. I mean, look at me. I examine myself in the mirror. Still wearing blouses and skirts that were fashionable – no, not even fashionable but respectable – twenty years ago. I am dressed in what plump middle-class middle-aged church-going housewives with no pretension to looks wear to camouflage their existence. Dowdy, frumpy. Is that me?

What are women wearing these days? I study the streams of consumers moving through the Darwin and Pride Hill shopping centres. A bewildering miscellany of outfits, from trousers and jeans to strange little T-shirt tops cut off just below the bosom, to reveal inches of midriff. Fluorescent light and garish music beat on my senses as I look for new clothes that will make a statement.

To and fro I pad from rail to closet, enacting bizarre metamorphoses. Eventually, sweating, I settle on extra large T-shirts and size 16 black trousers and a track suit. Having lost weight, I'm down by a whole size, and heading towards 14. 14 is average. 12 is slim. 10 is skinny. The new Jessie aims to be average body-weight. And to become, if not conspicuous, visible.

My father would have been scandalised at the trousers. I've never worn trousers in my life.

Male-impersonator, shouted my father at my sister, shaking with fury, when she came home with a pair of slacks.

Anyhow, shouted Ellen over the banister, *Jesus wore a skirt. So.* And she slammed the door and bolted it from inside.

As my mother's daughter, I never even considered wearing trousers. My bottom was too big anyway.

I'll need a new haircut to go with all this clobber.

When I come out of Plumage on Dogpole, scalped, I scurry along with my head down and collapse with my pile of purchases in Sivori's. The dimpled copper table-top reflects a fierce-faced modern who seems to say: anyone who objects to the way I look should leave now. When I reach an experimental hand to my scalp, the half-inch hair feels like a soft-bristled shaving-brush.

It feels light.

It feels like a statement.

But I need a pair of dangly ear-rings.

Stride back down Dogpole with twin cabbage-white butterflies dancing at my ears.

Brenda gives a small scream: 'What have you done to yourself?'

'It's the new me . . . what do you think?'

'Very nice, dear. Quite . . . what's the word? – affirm-ative? Assertive. Yes, I like it very much.'

'Well, you'll get used to it, love.'

I consider the new me in the bathroom mirror. Actu-ally, there's very little grey in the nearly black hair. It could never be a pretty face. Too much jaw. I practise the lion-impersonation with which I so greatly impressed Averil. Punch upwards with my fist and give a great bellowing roar, as instructed. The lampshade swings wildly. The butterflies likewise.

Oh Jessie, you're not fat, you're womanly, you're Rubenesque, Jacob used to say when I moaned about being overweight. *Come here and let me cuddle all that womanliness.*

Inside me there was always a willowy creature, supple and lissom, the feminine counterpart to Jacob.

But she was the diaphanous dream of an overweight wife.

Inside Jessie, yes, there is another Jessie indwelling, but sturdy and muscular, leonine, who now utters another somewhat feebler roar.

I turn away, feeling a fool.

Nothing from Jacob. He must be thinking over the contents of my letter.

The night was treacherous. I tried to ride its terrors with a philosophic mind, hard-come-by in the small hours when the body's chemistry betrays one to naked knowledge without protective clothing. Sitting up, I tried to pray, reminding myself about the lilies of the field and the fall of the sparrow. Every hair of my head he vowed was numbered. He wouldn't have lied about that. 'If it were not so, do you think I would not have told you?' It racked me that I rate Jesus' promises as tenuous as Jacob's; the latter's counterfeits have made the former seem a heaven away, beyond my scope. I lay wrestling with that for an hour or more; then got up and light was not yet evident through the landing window. Snapping on the bathroom light, I caught sight of a stubbled head in the cabinet mirror, a shorn black lamb. Who could love you, Jessie? Could Christ?

I saw a woman with dark and heavy eyebrows, somewhat lifted in a double arch of anxiety – the sort of

eyebrows most women pluck as unfeminine. I felt ...
disgraced. But what should *I* feel guilty about?

Yet guilt harrowed me as, wrapping my dressing-
gown round me, I crept downstairs to make some tea.

Now then, said the new Jessie. Now then, none of
that.

The old Jessie had run on this fuel of guilt for four
decades. Slouched over the slow-boiling kettle with an
empty hot water bottle under one arm, I realised how
far back it went.

– You'll not get rid of it now, said the old Jessie. You
know that. Better give in at once and stop this panto-
mime of pretending that you can break out and break
away. You well know what you have to feel guilty about,
she went on, and I passionately wished for dawn to
come; look at the way you've behaved to poor May,
even down to the petty meanness of resenting doing
Mrs Jenkins' washing.

– A woman who has no kin of her own.

Am I my brother's keeper?

– Yes, you are.

My mother-in-law's? My aunt-in-law's? My husband's mistress's baby's?

– Yes, you are.

I filled my hot water bottle and a pot of tea; took
them upstairs, trailing in the wake of all my journeys
bearing sustenance to others.

It's not living. It's never been living.

– But you've been happy, remonstrated the old Jessie.
If you'd been asked, you'd have said you were a happy
woman. Fulfilled.

I wasn't fulfilled, but I thought I was. Now that this
illusion no longer filmed my eye, I saw only the blank
stare of a guilt-riddled woman who'd fallen headlong
out of love with her fellow creatures.

It will seem different tomorrow.

Please, please let it.

And yet it's this constant shifting and swinging between moods that confounds me. If last night's guilty unease had been final and invariable, I could have started planning, accommodating once again to stooping under a low ceiling and subordinating my own needs to those of May and Brenda. Ploughing the old barren furrows summer and winter, winter and summer. A palimpsest of fruitless journeyings.

– But who in God's name wants to be buried alive? the new Jessie blazed in my head, she denied there was any point in going on living under these conditions . . . she might as well be dead. If she were dead, Jacob would just bloody well have to cope.

'What you need,' says Brenda, 'is a trampette.'

'Pardon?'

'You know, like a miniature trampoline. For fitness. Peter Fox has one, he swears by it. Why don't you ask him if you can have a go on his and see how it suits you?'

'Have a croissant. But why do you think I ought to have a trampette?'

'It would go so well with that new tracksuit. I can just see you on one. Peter says he does one hundred leaps at the start of every day, it releases all tensions, he says, and leaves you spry and uplifted.'

In the mirror last night I saw my own darkness, the underside of my mind. This morning, after glowing dreams of I'm-not-sure-what, it has lightened, and as I put on one of my new outfits, I tell myself that it's going to take a while . . . be kind to yourself . . . go with the tide. Jog. Row. Trampette if necessary, bouncing on the spot.

I suggest to Brenda that it would be no bad idea if she bounced gently out of bed and took a stroll round the house: the doctor counselled against becoming bed-bound. It would waste her bones more rapidly, he'd predicted, and increase the pain in the long term.

'Oh, Jessie, do I have to?' she asks in a childish voice.

'Of course not. You should please yourself, Brennie, it's your life. But I don't want you to be in worse pain.'

'It's odd, Jessie, the pain is less since I began to ... drift, and say to myself that active life is basically over.'

Although her voice is devoid of self-pity, this seems such a melancholy thing to say that I lift the tray off her bedclothes and take both her hands.

'Hey, Brennie, don't say that. I mean, look at Nathan, he's even getting married again.'

'No – you're not with me, I don't mean it like that. My time of day being twilight ... is neither good nor bad ... it's just how it is. You, being young, may not understand that.'

Always before, I'd seen the joggers on the opposite bank as another breed, loping or limping on their way in their designer togs, past the mums with toddlers and the dog-lovers, the gliding mountain-bikers. I had liked to see them run, as I peeled potatoes at the kitchen window, admired the easy gait of the young and smiled at the efforts of those past their peak. Now, rather embarrassed, I was to join them. But I strode to Greyfriars and crossed the bridge briskly, to warm up; rounded the corner down to the river and took to my heels – slowly, not pushing it – until, coming abreast of our house, I paused. Across the river, where the light flashed on our windows, I seemed to look back in retrospect to the guessed face of the woman I had been when walled up in the happiness of my marriage and the round of my cares.

This woman could not be revisited. Already I was outsiderly, separated by a whole river from her.

– There is a sadness in taking my leave of you, woman of shadows. Indoor woman with beaming smiles beaconing round and many hands pulling at your skirts. You were a film projected of other people's needs; you were designed to fill those needs, like a statue breathed into by a team of crafty sculptors.

– You were a wonderful invention. A universal lap.

All your rickety children throve.

Did they?

– There was something so ... smug and false ... as you half-knew, in your motherly fussing.

The old Jessie would tie people to her by the tightest possible bondings and make herself indispensable to them. I suddenly see myself as Jacob must have, so many times, repressing and controlling everyone; squeezing the life out of them, in the name of love.

They've done rather well without you.

Jacob's got himself a blonde. And a licorice allsorts family of children.

Nathan's found an ancient bride.

May is playing to a packed house.

Brennie's high on Zen.

Could it be that you weren't quite so necessary after all?

Thumping past the tennis courts, and round the bend into the Quarry, I shake off the memories. Am already deciding to bear right into town to stoke up on coffee.

'What's going on?' I asked Peter on Pride Hill.

'They're testifying,' he explained. Quite a crowd had massed between the town cross and Burger King, around the benches on which stood an elect cluster of souls amongst whom I recognised Deborah Pym, Ben Theology, Evie and others not known by name. Immune to muffled mirth and more open catcalls, they were narrating to the citizens of Shrewsbury the circumstances of their conversions.

'Goodness,' I said. 'Aren't they brave?'

'Braver than me,' said Peter. 'I can't manage that kind of thing, speechifying and so on. I wonder if I ought to try ... do you think?'

'I shouldn't,' I said. 'There are talkers and there are doers. You happen to be a doer. It's bearing witness just the same.'

'Dear Jessie ...' He looked grateful. Deborah was telling, in hectoring tones, of how she had experienced the Divine Light whilst being driven at thirty miles per hour in a green Morris Minor along the road to Much Wenlock in the winter of 1953. She and her companion, now alas dead, had parked there and then, and, walking out into a ploughed field, heedless of a spanking frosty wind, had sung out loud an impromptu hymn of praise.

'And,' continued Deborah, 'what will impress you as the scientific proof of God's call that chilly afternoon in November, is the fact that, when we opened our mouths to sing, *we both knew the words*.'

'Blimey,' said a bystander. 'A miracle.'

'Miraculous indeed, young man, is the forbearance and charity which My Saviour has shown to me a sinner.'

'Wow,' said another voice. 'I mean, is she real? She just wows me. She is something else.'

'A Plymouth Brother,' murmured the man beside me, in explanation to his wife of the evangelical phenomenon.

'Who's a Brother?'

157

'She is.'

'Shouldn't she be a Sister?'

'No, they're all under the umbrella of Brothers. You can tell by the hairstyle she's one of the Brethren.'

'It's not a Devon accent,' the wife objected.

'Goodness me, woman, you don't need to come from Plymouth to be a Brother,' replied her spouse testily.

'Well, why shouldn't she be called a Much Wenlock Brother then? Though Sister would be more ... rational.'

'Oh my sainted aunt, give over, will you.'

'And now,' announced Deborah, 'the youngest sheep in our little fold will give his testimony.'

In expectation of some precocious seven-year-old, I was disappointed at the emergence of Ben, a person trading on a long-outlived reputation for youthfulness. He doesn't even look particularly young any longer. His beard predicts a career in prophecy.

The detailed notes with which Ben organised his spontaneity flapped in the wind as he described the intellectual rigour with which he had addressed the question of Truth since the age of eleven. But by four-teen, he had been growing mystified and jaded: no learned doctor in Wem, his home town, could satisfy his thirst for knowledge. Then he experienced the pres-ence of the Spirit in so compelling a manner that the force had almost plunged him beneath water-level (he being in the bath), baptising him by total immersion. And since that day he had known true Rapture, at which several persons in the crowd shouted 'Praise The Lord!' and a lad wearing the scarf of Shrewsbury Town threw a beer can in the air and whooped in derision.

While Deborah in a businesslike way was inviting the unsaved to come up and declare for Christ, including in her invitation any backsliding sons or daughters who might care to take the opportunity of renewing their pledges, Peter and I sidled off.

'Well,' said Peter, at the junction between Mardol and Pride Street, 'she's a very well-meaning woman.'

'True,' I agreed.

'But you ... haven't you changed your hairstyle or something, Jess?'

'It's my new image.' I didn't expect him to approve.

'Fascinating.' And he looked fascinated. I'd felt his eyes performing covert inspections at intervals during the meeting. 'Athletic. Personally, I was never much good at games. Awkward, caggy-handed. Which of course is no fun for a boy. I think it set me apart rather.'

'Brenda says you have a trampette in your back room,' I reminded him wickedly. 'She says you secretly bounce.'

'Oh yes, it's great fun. Come home and have a look-see. Do.'

Hawthorn was in full flower, and boughs spilled over with cherry blossom, in the lavish gardens of Peter's avenue. In this Edwardian house he had lived with his father until his death several years ago; never married. Had been, I know, devoted to his father, and I remember his telling me with tears in his eyes how they had been 'like one person', a statement I heard with awe. I could not fathom such an affinity, though I could credit it, seeing them gardening together on summer afternoons, both in their shirt-sleeves, the youthful-looking father and the prematurely middle-aged son; the father lifting seedlings from their peaty beds for the kneeling son to plant. And how they looked up and greeted me with a kindred expression in their short-sighted eyes. And later, when the father was ninety and recovering from his penultimate stroke, the son would carry him out to direct pruning and weeding. *I always felt he'd died too soon*, Peter had lamented, where most people would perhaps have felt that ninety-one was a decent innings.

My mother and his father had been close, exchanging slips and cuttings, together with bulletins of how they prospered. My garden and Peter's therefore have sundry ancestors in common and, though we lack our parents' know-how and the Latin plant-names that delight and distinguish the cognoscenti, we can recognise in one another's plots a common inheritance.

Yet I had never been drawn to Peter. Something of his generalised benignity seemed to exclude the genuinely personal, and, yes, he had supplied the word, there was a caggy-handedness to his dealings which gave some of his behaviour a faintly inane quality. I had sometimes reproached myself for this unworthy feeling.

Perhaps I had been saying to myself all along that he was not as manly as Jacob.

But now, when he settled me in the easy chair next to the window, from which I could see the blossom-laden boughs of his prunus trees, and bustled to and fro setting a tray with willow-pattern cups and plates, all I saw was the gentleness and courtesy of his welcome. I rested my head against the embroidered shepherdess in a field of lavender silks, and passively allowed myself to be served.

'Now, I shall draw up this coffee-table, so, and you're warm enough? . . . I can't tell you how happy it makes me, Jessie, to have you here. Do you know,' he said as he poured my tea, 'I've always been slightly in awe of you, Jessie.'

'I can't imagine why.'

'I suppose I've always thought of you as rather an intellectual.'

'You're joking, Peter. I don't even have time to read

a book these days. In fact, I don't know when I last did read a book.'

'Yes, but you would be reading a book if you had the time for it.'

'Goodness, is that how you see me?' I coloured up: it was as if a window had been opened on to a self of mine that had either got lost or suffered atrophy along the way. A self I'd not glimpsed for ... how many years? And there was a sweetness to that image, which flattered me. Whereas I had been yawningly sure he was about to congratulate me on my self-sacrificial qualities, he surprised me by reminding me that there was a self to be sacrificed.

'Perhaps it's that I used to be a librarian,' I suggested. 'You've seen me against a background of books – but you probably didn't register that it's a cardinal sin for a librarian to be caught reading.'

'No – no, it isn't that. Have a scone, I made them myself yesterday. And some damson jam, it's quite more-ish. No, Jessie, it's a quality you have – of something deeper. Actually very sharp. I'm sure Jacob felt this. Whoops!' and he clapped his hand to his mouth in mid-chew. 'Foot in it again. Typical.'

'How do you mean, Jacob felt that?'

'Oh, that you – in every sense – passed him by, him being a joiner ... don't be offended, Jessie, just ignore me blabbering on.'

'I'm not offended, Peter, it's just that I don't think he or anyone except you, bless you, sees me like that. Ellen was the intellectual sister, I was the practical one. That was how we were programmed. You see, I never saw any difference between Jacob and me – he was just my ... life. That was what I thought.' I turned my face away and meditated aloud. 'But apparently it was not so.' And the mantelpiece clock echoed 'Not so.' I went

161

on, 'I cast about for reasons but I don't find them. I mean, maybe it comes down to something as simple as that I wasn't as attractive for a woman as he is for a man so we weren't ... counterparts ... and maybe life's as crude as that, I've lost him to a fitter, more fertile specimen – sexual selection, as in Darwin ... I used to pass his statue every morning going into work. It was either something very deep or it was something very shallow, or it was just something in the nature of things, like weather.'

He did not say anything but, putting his tea-cup carefully, almost primly, on the tray, came over in his slippers to my chair and knelt by my side. Relieving me of my cup, which he placed side-by-side with his, he took me in both arms and hugged me. I did not query Peter's motivation or feel in any way abashed or invaded. I let myself be gathered in to his pale blue lambswool pullover, laying my head with a sigh on his shoulder, feeling his big, reassuring body against mine.

It was utterly wonderful.

Nor did it feel odd when we removed to his immaculately made bed, and he drew aside the duvet and stood aside for me, with a courtly gesture as if ushering me through a door ahead of him. I lay down, fully clothed, in the veiled light, and he lay down beside me, holding me tightly but carefully, collecting my flying-asunder self together and recomposing its disintegration.

I almost slept. He seemed familiar. He seemed known. He seemed as unlike Jacob as it was possible to be.

Then he brought me another cup of tea.

We drank together and dunked gingerbread biscuits: more gingery than any I had ever tasted. And as we shared these moments, it came over me to wonder (glancing sidelong at his munching jaw) if Peter did this all the time: bringing his needy cases home to administer to them his hands-on healing? Brenda's saying, in regard to his trampolining, 'You never know what people get up to in the privacy of their own homes' came back to me, and I giggled.

'It's nice to hear you laugh,' he said earnestly.

'I was thinking about the trampette,' I said. 'We never did get round to having a bounce.'

'Next time you come,' he promised, like a shot, 'we shall definitely make a point of it.'

And even if he did this all the time, conferring his quiet blessings on one and all, I said to myself that it didn't matter. He'd done me good. Touch was so beautiful, substantiating. More important almost than anything. And he hadn't pushed me beyond what I wanted, or exacted anything: he'd given. I'd always dimly conceived of him as homosexual, probably non-practising. Or an eternal virgin, arrested in his development. But he was neither. He was gentle, generous.

As I got up, still fully clothed, I glowed all over my body, light gleaming from my comforted skin to my soul as if through high windows into a vault.

'Nathan said Jacob never made me a cup of tea,' I told him. 'You've made me two in one afternoon.'

'It is an honour to be allowed to make Jessie Copplestone a cup of tea,' he said with a certain stiff gallantry which again set off a giggle. 'Well, it is. Have another.'

'I couldn't. I'm awash.'

Of course it will lead nowhere. I don't want it to. I meandered back along the town walls. The feeling of levity was wonderful. Peter stood stretching at his front door, yawning as if he'd just awoken. The Severn was misty, its vague light seeming to soften my eye's horizons with the sense of unpredictable possibilities. I've touched the world again and found it still real and solid.

'Have a nice jog, dear?' asked Brenda.

'Brilliant.'

'Don't overdo it. You're not used to the exercise.'

Chapter 11

Nathan has married his gentle, strong-minded Quaker: Catherine and I sat with Dorothy's brother in the Registry Office, the businesslike service taking place in the first slot of the morning, so that the couple were all done and dusted, as Dorothy expressed it, by 10.30 a.m. Impossible not to be at once touched and tickled by their mutual joy, Nathan abdicating his stick to stand quiveringly upright before the Registrar, pledging his vows with a firm voice. As they stood there hand-in-hand, the complex tears ran down my face; for it is equally impossible to deny that the sight of other people's fulfilment brings a pang, or shadow, of out-siderliness.

Dorothy is physically still rather impressive, though she must be in her mid-seventies. She stands very straight, giving the impression of height. Her hair is not exactly grey or white, but a beautiful silver, drawn back into a bun from her thin, austere face. I was sure I'd met her somewhere before but could not place her. I stored up every detail to tell Brenda, who continues frail.

Nathan was passionately keen that we should like and accept one another.

'My niece – my very special niece,' he kept repeating, and, 'Yes,' said Dorothy, 'I know – I first saw you out rowing (we were sitting by the statue of Hercules, such an uncouth chap, I always think, with that horrid club), and Nathan became so excited waving to you that the thought occurred that he might jump in and try to swim across to you, like Hero and Leander.'

'Goodness, how embarrassing. It was my first-ever row.'

'And I said to Dorothy,' put in Nathan, holding her hand and my arm, 'you must meet my dear niece; she and Brenda and dear May are all I have now of true family – and she said, I should like that indeed. You had shot into a willow tree at the time – and you were resting on your oars, half in and half out, and then you freed yourself from the net of branches and pulled strongly out into the river, looking over your shoulder, and you made a wide arc and turned. I said to Dorothy "Look at her go". A solo voyage.'

'A maiden voyage,' I said. 'I enjoyed it but unfortunately the poor old boat is falling to pieces.'

Nathan told me over a glass of sparkling wine and an egg and cress sandwich, that he had spoken at length to Dorothy of his first wife, to whom he still feels a loyalty, but who had been entirely different from his new bride. Dorothy received all confidences in an unjudging spirit, cherishing the faith that each and every person has an inner light, from which she can learn.

I privately wondered what spark she'd have managed to discern in her sombre, meagre predecessor. I'd never taken to Bethan, who came from a strict background, her father (Welsh Tabernacle tradition) having been prominent in the Lord's Day Observance Society.

'Not even knitting was allowed,' Nathan explained to his new wife, ' – and Bethan was a consummate knitter, so there was a sacrifice involved there.'

'Is that one of her creations you're wearing now, Nathan?'

'It is.'

'It's very smart.' Dorothy praised his speckled three-ply waistcoat. 'Your dear wife was evidently a talented woman.'

'She was, Dorothy, but most of all she was godly. For Sunday lunch it was cold cuts – no cooking allowed on the sabbath, you see. Of course this had its drawbacks. Not for me, you understand, since I could occupy myself very happily in prayer and Biblical readings – but when her relatives came (she was blessed with a copious family), the children must sit quiet as mice with their hands in their laps – no profane skipping or anything that Bethan thought would take their minds off the sanctity of the day.'

'Well,' said Dorothy with a fractional hesitation, 'that's certainly one way of spending the Lord's day. Perhaps not everyone's cup of tea – for me, I think a little more in the way of fizz gives me the sabbath feel.'

She swirled the wine in her glass and took a decisive sip.

'Oh, fizz would not have done for Bethan. Coca Cola Christianity she'd have called that. Our greatest indulgence was to sing a psalm together at eventide to see out the day.'

'You will find me lax, I'm afraid, Nathan, in point of observance – and radical as to politics – and of course our meetings are mere silence.'

'*I* know where we've seen you before, Dorothy,' I exclaimed. 'You were there when the Peace Group laid the white poppy wreath at the War Memorial in the Quarry last year.'

'I was indeed! And were you there too?'

'Yes, Catherine and me – don't you remember, Cathy,

Dorothy was one of the people who actually placed the wreath, after the Remembrance Day march-pasts and so on – and there was such a row with the British Legion afterwards.'

'Didn't they call it a hi-jack?' asked Catherine.

'That's right, dear, they did,' said Dorothy. 'It saddens me beyond words to think they feel insulted, when all we're really doing is to remember all the forgotten victims of war – all the civilians, the refugees, the traumatised children ... and they don't realise we're not attacking the Forces mourners, we're saying "Peace *without* the trappings of militarism". They just don't realise, you see; they shouldn't feel hurt.'

I gazed at Nathan: whatever would Bethan have said at this audacious spirit my uncle was marrying? Evidently he had not a qualm in the world. His eyes rested on her face, speaking so vehemently, in the perfect trust that nothing she said could be untruth. I squeezed his hand, and tears rose to my eyes again, this time unalloyed with envy. Nathan is evidently willing to adjust his theology whichever way she gestures; and has given up being teetotal in sign of his new allegiance.

In fact he grew nicely tipsy; sang a verse of 'O love that wilt not let me go', and took a surprise nap, at which Dorothy said, 'Bless him,' and observed that it had been an exciting morning.

As we leave, the thorn in my mind embeds itself a little deeper. They will have one another. Cathy will go home to her darlings. A cold dislike of my fellow humans comes and goes with aches and shivers; I hate it, despise myself for feeling it. Something dark and ugly in the centre of my soul is coming through to the surface, where I can't ignore it. It wrings me now as Cathy picks up Joe, who's whimpering, and raises him above her, wiggling his fat body in the air, where he crows, and she talks nonsenses to him, as face to face, they mirror one another; and I am the dark other, beyond the mirror, looking on, looking in. Neither Peter's big hugs (which I am avoiding with distaste) nor Catherine's part-time solidarity can lighten this stupefying load of malignity.

'What is it, love?' asks Cathy. She has antennae; seldom misses the flicker of an expression.

'Oh – nothing.'

'Yes, there is. What?'

'Nothing. Really.'

'Let's bung Joe in the back of the car and scoot off somewhere. Shall we? Where shall we go? The Stiperstones?'

She hoists the baby into his carrycot, and dumps the wailing carrycot on the back seat.

Climbing in to the front, I buckle my seat belt but murmur, 'I don't want to interfere with . . . your family things.'

'Don't be daft. It will be brilliant to get out together. I feel as if we've spent far too little time together. Sorry about all these crisp papers and stuff, just chuck it in the back.' And she chunters on about how lovely Dorothy is.

But then everyone in Catherine's universe is lovely. And if they demonstrably aren't, that's because misfortune has been too much for them. They would have been lovely if they could. Probably they have once been and somehow lost the knack or had it stolen by a rapacious society.

Perhaps nothing has more deeply imprinted the sense of Jacob's trespass than Cathy's condemnation of him: *I'd like to castrate that bastard* still rings in my ears.

'Have you had any more news?' she asks gently, as

we drive towards Pontesbury, the velvet mound of the hill preluding the rugged spine of the Stiperstones.

'A lawyer's exchange, that's all.'

I don't specify. The feeling is too complex and raw. Aware of Cathy's querying glance, I avert my head and stare at the green back of Pontesbury Hill. Cannot forgive myself for my behaviour to May, which violates every principle I've ever lived for. Have thrown Jacob and Hazel even more firmly into a couple by wishing his unwanted mother on them. Apparently Jacob is outraged that I have refused responsibility for his mother. He feels swindled. I have betrayed my solemn undertaking, is how he puts it: and though this seems, and is, preposterous from a man of his infidelity, part of me feels so grubby and corrupt as to prove his point. He is now demanding in settlement half the house, as he will have the expensive responsibility of putting May in a home, and, since I have elected to retrain and go back to work, is showing reluctance to maintain me, despite the fact that I am caring for his aunt.

Tristan Pugh, my solicitor, says he's trying it on. 'Don't worry, Mrs Copplestone, we'll just drag our heels – since your husband is going all out for a quick divorce, he'll soon see reason.'

The formal letters, written in the cool dialect of legalese, are searing; more so than the hottest confrontation. This cannot be Jacob; cannot be me. So many woven years of careful love unravelling so rapidly, as we each pull for advantage. The sprightly dialogue between the old Jessie and the new Jessie has lost all cogency in this horror of loss and self-betrayal.

For I was designed thousands of years ago; shaped to fill a certain use and to derive my sense of worth from that function. There is absurdity in trying to change my destiny and to escape the conscience they've implanted like a mechanical heart that beats an imperative, day and night, overriding wishes, desires and ambitions. All I am capable of hearing is that implanted motor. Perhaps younger women can realistically hope to slip these shackles fitted at birth like bracelets as accessories to our pink frocks; but as I confront myself in the mirror, with my modishly aggressive haircut, my thrusting jaw, all I see is a panicked creature, defiantly cornered. Sooner or later she will creep back to her position, resume her multiple burden and keep her head down.

'What I find hardest to cope with,' I tell Catherine, 'is the mood-swings. One morning I feel quite strong . . . and the next . . . just pathetic.' I don't admit that I also feel queasily in the wrong. It will set her off on the quarrel we had at Chad's when I explained to her I was programmed and she gave the unwanted advice – and I'll resent her.

I don't want to resent her. It's so unfair, she loves me and I love her. But Cathy doesn't need me as I need her. Necessarily, she is diluted, spread so thin; and there is something so bitter in me that it curdles my perceptions.

' "I am gall, I am heartburn",' I say, quoting Hopkins. 'You wouldn't understand that.'

' "I am gall, I am heartburn",' she takes it up; ' "God's most deep decree/ Bitter would have me taste; my taste was me." I wish you didn't feel like that, Jessie.'

'It will go off,' I murmur, without conviction.

'Oh, it will. I know it will. You're bound to feel like death.'

That is indeed how I feel, like death. It beckons, seduces, from the deepest shadows.

Last night I rang the number of the Samaritans in the early hours. Of course I crashed the phone down before they had a chance to answer. I sat and shook: me, calling the Samaritans – me, Jessie Copplestone, the woman who could never pass by on the other side – me, calling for help. I reflected, when I'd calmed, on the come-down of joining the eleven thousand people of this town who have rung the Samaritans in the last twelve months. Eleven thousand of us, so many of me, all sealed in incommunicado capsules of despair.

No-hopers. Lost souls. I felt ashamed. And ashamed of my shame. I huddled under my duvet, with a hot water bottle against my stomach, though it is June and very warm; and felt my mind curdle, against Jacob, against Nathan and his ridiculous playing at bride-grooms, against my darling Catherine, husbanded, shepherding her lambs. In my mind's eye I could see her with the cello she's had to put by since the babies came (because they climb it and try to enter or vandalise it, as a competitor for her attention): Cathy playing her heart out, her pale hair's silky tendrils so soft beside the powerful feminine body of the instrument. A contralto woman, playing in the deepest reaches of our range.

I have been too quick, all my adult life, to offer hand-outs of fellow feeling. Dispense pills of advice; offer cakes of wisdom, pre-baked. I, who had all the recipes, knew damn-all. Now I know how it feels to be amongst the eleven thousand, I am cringingly aware of the vanity of my past do-goodings. I deserve this.

I sicken myself.

Slitting my wrists does not appeal, and besides there would be the trauma for the person who had to clear up the mess.

Leaping from one of the bridges: some interfering busy-body would jump in and lynch me out, half-drowned, and imagine the despair of being brought back to one's duty to be alive and on call. Besides I'm lacking in even a normal ration of physical courage.

Probably the sleeping pills and plastic bag over the head.

This thought is so comforting that I involuntarily smile; and her alert eyes catch the change of expression, so that she turns her head and smiles too, relieved that my dark mood is lightening. I love her the more unbearably in that she ties me to life: how can I bear to hurt her by taking off – saying, in so many words, in the end your friendship is not enough to keep me here.

'Oh, Cathy – I'm so sorry.'

'For – what?'

'I don't know. I don't know. I'm sorry in advance.'

'We will come through this.' She says *we*. She is careful to say *we* and to inflect it so that I know she places herself in the same space with me.

'Yes.'

'We will. Look, we're through Pennerley, the Bog should be coming up any time now. Keep your eye out.'

On the west flank of the long hill, the disused lead mines come and go; we veer left and mount to the Stiperstones carpark.

She is strapping Joe into the sling on her chest and I am looking out over the glorious ridge of hills in an intense quiet. I call it quiet although the sheep are bleating for miles and the wind sheers in – but still I perceive a silence, looking out across the green slopes to the Welsh hills. Cloudscapes for miles, powerful and dramatic, lift my spirits from sullen brooding, as the tracts of blueness above, bearing patches of cotton wool cloud and a single hang-glider, pass into stormy zones of dense grey cloud, perforated by silver beams over the remote hills.

The foaming of ferns as we climb the stile and begin to climb.

The stippling of colour, russet, green and grey, a

wilderness of heather and bilberry, and the ochre remnant of last year's bracken, over the hillside.

Plantation of evergreens to the east and a single bird playing the air-currents above acres of gorse.

Turfy path so soft beneath our feet.

Earthly beauty: how could I bear to leave you?

Wind up our sleeves, scalding our faces, secret on the thin skin of our palms; Joe right and tight inside your billowing anorak. Shall I take him?

Joe now slung round my neck and back, looks puzzled, with raised eyebrows, as he examines the rust-red interior of my jacket, my black milkless bosom; but he's snug enough. She floats off free of his weight and waves as I toil behind. The tors resemble man-made ruins, houses reduced to rubble in some blitz, chimneys still standing on the last of a bombed-out roof. Behind sun-burnished Cathy toils her long shadow, as she passes a burnt-away mass of heather like some old woman's rough silver-grey hair, shining in the light.

She turns to wave: 'Come on! It's great!' As children, she'd always dive in first while I tested a toe at the shallow end.

Up here on the ridge, the wind is slamming, and Joe doesn't know what to think. I cup his head and behind in both hands and whisper messages to where he hides in me, and beam, and his smile gleams back. Cathy thinks this tor is the Devil's Chair, but I'm sure it's the Cranberry Tor. Who cares? We christen them all Devils' Chairs, from which Satan surveys his terrain, looking out over the whole county and into Wales, which we view along his eyeline like an aerial photo. Each tor is a fist of quartzite thrust up from the upturned strata in the Ice Age, when freezes and thaws folded up the ridge and shattered the rock, which lies as gleaming scree all down the westward slope.

Having taken in the panorama, we retire to the sheltered side of the tor, lying out with our heads on bilberry bushes, loving it.

Thin winds come sweeping up the moorland, like someone whistling between his teeth. We cloud-watch, the earth solid beneath our spines, and see how the misty wreathings of clouds twist inside-out as they travel slowly across our field of blue vision, in constant flow. And some detach from the main body and drift off into wispy gatherings which gradually disperse until there's just blueness, and a chalky smudge of what was once a cloud.

She feeds Joe as I cloud-watch. Then I prowl the ridge alone, scrambling from tor to tor, past a quartz impersonation of a sphinx, the gable-end of a fantastic house, the prow of a Viking boat. Over the bouldery moonscape I edge, wind-thrashed, with jagged rocks digging into my trainers; until, over miles of heather, from a new summit, I confront a black hill, cold under cloud-shadow, the geology of hell.

'It's like hell over there, it's wonderful,' I report back.

Behind Cathy and Joe, an aged couple are attempting to climb our Devil's Chair, in a worrying manner, considering the shaky brittleness of their legs and the way they claw on to one another, poking their walking sticks into fissures in the rock. To our relief they give up the ascent and discuss when and where they should eat their packed lunches.

'How will they ever get down?' Cathy wonders.

But, while we are lying on our backs cloud-watching again, they shin down rather nimbly, leaving us to an hour of sunny listlessness, listeners-in to Joe's liquid babble, the visiting bees' hum, an occasional bird.

Later, lounging down the turf carpet, the relaxation feels like a drug.

'Scatter my ashes up there,' I petition. 'Don't forget.'

'You mustn't go,' she says, and grasps one arm quite painfully.

'You don't need me, Cathy.' I say it as a matter of fact, without bitterness or wish to hurt.

'I do. I do need you.'

'But you've got – '

'Have you *no* idea?'

'What of?'

'You are . . . my closest-of-close . . . from the beginning. And,' she goes on challengingly, 'if you don't know that, all I can say is – my hair would all fall out again, if I lost you.'

Startled, I mull over this revelation. I remember it quite clearly, how during her teens – she must have been about thirteen – all Catherine's hair fell out in a week, so that she was completely bald. Somehow the idea of scalp and skull beneath our hair had always seemed rather hypothetical, until that week. *Alopecia*, said the doctor, promising *It will grow back again*. And it did – but a different colour, the pale colour between brown and blonde that it has remained. And whether it was an imbalance of nervous origin, or some freak of adolescence, or what, no one knew. How fiercely she bore herself, refusing the camouflage of a wig: her green Priory School uniform and that nude head shining in the sunlight.

She became for a while an unacknowledged pariah: people unconsciously sheering away from the mirror-image that anatomised them.

Back we drive through Pulverbatch, on the English side of the ridge. Joe, sound asleep on the back seat, emits a tiny droning snore; and I kiss her goodbye, running light fingers through her hair, with the assurance that she can keep it on this time.

*

The phone is ringing when I get in; and I curse it, through the urge to deposit my drowsy inertia in a hot bath, with a mug of steaming tea, and the tape of the Dvorak quintet. I've set up this luxurious scenario in my imagination, so vividly as to feel the warm water lapping round my body, the sweep of the music at my temples.

On the edge of the bath I shall balance a plate of bourbon biscuits, which I shall dip into the tea and suck.

'Jess, it's Jacob.' Businesslike voice; no polite prelude.

He wants me to know that he has been to see May.

Oh. And?

'You don't seem very interested,' he complains. 'You were the one who took her in and now you don't seem to care whether she lives or dies.'

Small matter of his leaving her, me, aunt, uncle, the whole lot, in the soup.

Quite a different matter, apparently: he has a family of small children to consider, plus a baby on the way, and a partner who is not well at all. They went to the hospital this morning and she is to have a scan.

So?

May refuses point-blank to go into a home.

So what are you going to do about that, Jacob?

'You will have to take over the whole business, Jessica. I'm far too busy and tied up.'

She's your mother.

'She's your responsibility, Jess, as you well know. You made it your business to minister to her as your life's work – never mind how it ruined my life into the bargain. You know that. You know it as well as I do. I've told the hospital social worker and the OT to get on to you and that you will make arrangements for her discharge. I suggest that you take her back on the old arrangements and then see what you want to do. In those circumstances I would obviously waive my claim on the house.'

How dare he?

'That's all for now. I'll be in touch.'

'Right,' I say. 'No divorce.'

'If you don't grant me this divorce, under the agreed terms, I will make life very tough for you, Jessie, I can promise you that.'

I laugh out loud, with a sort of bray.

'You appal me, Jacob,' I tell him. 'You have turned into . . . into a – an utter – cad.'

Now it's his turn to laugh and enquire what old-fashioned books I've been reading? Have I the least idea what it has been like to live for twenty years with one of the most sanctimonious sexless killjoy prigs in the whole of the Midlands?

Do tell me more, I urge, but a certain nightmarish horror is rising in my mind; the certainty that I had better put the phone down now, while there's time, and not hear any more.

I do so, and push back the lever that turns off the bell, to partition me not only from Jacob but from all interventions with the world beyond my walls. Chaining the door, I pull the front room curtains so that no one can spy me out.

Peter called . . . he called several times after that afternoon . . . but I shivered (all goose-flesh) in recoil from the intimacy of his voice, and spoke of the remotest themes that came to mind, such as my sister's trip to Florida. He asked if he had offended me, or been insensitive, caggy-handed? Of course not, I replied; no indeed, in that prim, tight voice with which Jacob must often have been greeted, when I was dead-beat after a day of May's capers.

Peter said, sounding hurt ... if ever, I mean if ever you need me, be in touch.

I feel like dregs, left-overs. After that high-flying day, that high-aimed life, I come down to this rueful shambling past Brenda's bedroom door with a subdued hello, into the bathroom, where I strip off sweaty clothes, and rub my skin pink-raw with the loofah.

It's strange though, there's relief in caving in, and how suddenly this collapse happens, seeming inevitable; to have been inevitable all the time. If I crawl out of this mess back to my old way of life, everything will be easier even though infinitely more arduous, and soul-destroyingly boring. I'll appease my conscience; obey St Paul, please Jacob, obliquely support his partner, his baby, their new family, succour his old family. I'll be necessary again. No one will ask, *How could she leave them all in the lurch like that?*

I step out cleansed, shriven.

Yes, I vow as I towel myself vigorously dry, I will go back, I'll pick up and shoulder the burden again, wiser now for having been tempted, I'll learn to travel the way of love again; and find, as before, the compensations of the Cross, but with perhaps more genuine humility.

Yet my footsteps drag as I pad through to ask Brenda what she needs; and part of me burns as eros never did to have it all over and done, to be scattered ashes, quit of it all; them all. And the burning is anger. It is the well-remembered spasm of spite and bitterness in glancing out of the window at the unencumbered couples drifting along the opposite bank, while I smilingly put on my hobbling irons that no longer seem to fit, though they were once made to measure.

'So how was it?' asks Brenda.

'Oh – Nathan's wedding ... they were dear. So happy.'

'That's nice. You look rather green. Aren't you well?'

'Oh, I'm okay. Just a touch of dyspepsia.'

'Take some Alka Salzer.'

'I will.'

Ringing the social worker, and discussing May's release, a flat gloom supersedes the confusion of emotions that have weltered in me over these weeks. I find myself slipping automatically into the role I'd played so many years, gentle, biddable, wishing for the greatest good of the greatest number. Showing concern not only for May but for the social worker herself, who does not neglect this opportunity of revealing the pressures and obstacles to her job, caused by the NHS market-system, managers who shall be nameless, and even her younger daughter, who is a terrible worry to her.

'It must be grim for you,' I sympathise.

Oh it is, she doesn't know how she copes, but she supposes one just has to keep going. And thank heaven for people like yourself, Mrs Copplestone, the whole system would collapse without people like you.

When I put down the phone, it is with a certain quaking relief that I can still present that face of caring and coping: ashamed too, for there is a sharp, sardonic person behind the dove-mask. He ripped the mask away and exposed that hidden self-seeking misanthrope.

If one cannot love, I think to myself, ruefully, as I vacuum May's room, and make a list of items that must be got in for her return, and write a letter of notification to the DSS that she has left hospital, if one cannot love, the next best thing will be to act tenderly and forbearingly, and then the love may return, and action and sentiment be brought into accord.

Will it hell.

She'll be home on Monday.

I awaken headlong on Sunday, thinking *No*.

It seems impossible to abandon this peaceable life of freedom and normality for that suffocation and claustrophobia. I cling to the vestiges of my last day, lingering in the garden as the sun buries itself in the blackening yew-mass behind the limes.

The reluctance becomes so painful that I cannot enjoy the final evening; I wish May were back already so that I could readjust.

'You can't mean it,' says Cathy. She sounds vexed. But it's not her place to make judgements. She doesn't have to live my life.

'I do mean it.'

'But why?'

'Because I can't do otherwise.'

There is a pause. 'You're throwing your life away,' she observes. 'It's masochistic.'

'Thank you,' I reply sullenly.

'Look here, I didn't say you were a masochist, I just said it was ... oh for gosh sake, Jessie, break out of all that.'

'How would you like it if I told you to leave your babies and swan off to ... Spain or somewhere?'

'It's different. You know it's different. Please, Jessie, let Jacob deal with his own responsibilities.'

'Catherine, she's a *person*, not a responsibility. Look, you're not helping – do you mind if I just get on, I've got loads to sort out and I'm running behind.'

There is a choked sob at the other end, and she says, with an ache in her voice, 'I'd thought we were coming ... so close. Now you're putting yourself back into purdah ...'

'I'm grateful for all you've done, Cathy, love – I'll never forget it – '

'I don't want *gratitude*, I want ... oh, I don't know

what I want ... I suppose in the end I just want to know that you're all right.'

The conversation peters out in an exchange of kind, tired formulae.

Jane Venner rings to say that I'm a brick; and that if the brick ever needs a baby-sitter, not to forget her.

Brenda is flushed with agitation. Her furlough is also over, now that May is expected and all her incantations and sussurations are failing in efficacy.

Jacob cannot express how grateful he is. He tries, in a stammering of relief and praise for my wonderful character; he apologises for the daft things he's said, it was the stress apparently, getting him down, and they had a scare about the baby but luckily there was nothing in it.

A whacking great bouquet of flowers is delivered by Interflora more or less at cock-crow on Monday morning: 'With best wishes, Jacob.'

CHAPTER 12

May's arrival has been held up by the shortage of ambulances. I've been on the phone to the hospital, to be assured that 'Mrs Copplestone will be home by midday'. Mid-day came and went. Time passes in tithes of fractions of minutes, as I shuttle between window, phone, Brenda, the loo and the door, whenever the false hope of a vehicle draws up.

Brenda's agitation has revived her old demon of incontinence, or rather the fear of incontinence, dormant all these May-free weeks. She needs frequent assisted trips to the loo, where nothing much happens for extended periods.

I am frozen-calm, although a frenzied shadow of myself peels off and stamps in a riot of screaming round the house.

I am in control.

I am prepared to stand vigil here all day long if necessary. Fortunately I was designed as an automaton. I require neither food nor drink, except the black bitterness of the coffee with which I have been homeopathically medicining myself all morning.

'Now, it's all right, Brennie, you take your time, nothing to worry about,' I soothe. Realising that I'm standing to attention, like a guardsman outside his box, I take a deep breath, exhaling slowly, which Brenda interprets as a sigh of impatience, and says plaintively from inside the lavatory that she knows she's a nuisance, she wishes she'd died at seventy-one with her friend Nettie, she'll go into Ivanhoe with Nathan to take herself off my hands, with many, many etceteras, and apologies for the etceteras . . .

'Now, it's all right, Brennie, take your time, don't worry . . .'

Of course it was written in the stars that May's arrival would coincide with the critical phase of one of these expeditions, when Brenda has just managed to relax enough to disburden her painful bladder, a release which is ambushed by the 'Coo-ee' of the ambulance man round the door:

'Mrs Copplestone . . . ah, there you are, sorry we're late, dear, rather a lot of emergencies this morning . . . I'm afraid the other Mrs Copplestone refuses to get out of the ambulance – is demanding we drive her to the morgue and put her out of her misery. We've not had much success in persuading her.'

Brenda emits a long, low wail. Just as she had reached deliverance, her hydraulic system closes up.

'I tell you what we'll do, Brennie,' I say with cool decision. 'We'll get you back to the sitting room and a couple of Valium into you, to calm your nervous system.'

'But I don't believe in tranquillisers,' she objects.

'Brennie – please – believe in them for my sake. I've got to get May in and sorted out, and she's making a hullaballoo out there.'

Brenda, an instant and contrite convert, winces down into her chair and receives on her tongue the little yellow pills as an act of fellowship.

'Go on,' she says. 'Sorry, love.'

A cluster of neighbours around the open back of the

ambulance is attempting to coax May out. The greater the audience she attracts out there in the stifling heat, the better rewarded May becomes, and the more determined to remain in her refuge, which she compares with the sanctuary offered by a church to an illegal immigrant. The sight of my hovering self brings on a bout of name-calling vitriol which has the neighbours enthralled: where did she learn such language? Has she ever been in the army?

'Hello, Mum,' I greet her, making my way through the audience. 'We thought you'd never come.'

'Thought I'd never come! – that's a good one – hoped I'd never come, that's more like it – you don't want me home, you don't! *You* said you wouldn't have me!' She pronounces these words not to me but to the spectators, sizzling with dolorous triumph like a passionately frying rasher: '*I* know when I'm not wanted. Drive on,' she instructs the ambulance-crew. 'You-know-where. *She* doesn't want me.'

'Now come, come, Mrs Cop,' says the ambulanceman, in a friendly but misguided attempt at cajolery. 'Of course your daughter wants you. Look, she's standing here in the heat waiting to take you in.'

'Take me in? What do you think I am, a lost dog?'

'No, not that kind of taking-in, I mean . . .'

'Oh, I see, the other kind of taking-in. Well, I wasn't born yesterday, Mister, nobody takes May Copplestone for a ride.'

'In that case, Mrs Cop,' puts in the driver, in rather an adroit move, 'you'd better get down from there, or you *will* be taken for a ride – to Shelton Hospital, that's our next port of call.'

May, like a queen on progress, looks disgusted at the poor quality of the reception, haughtily flails her sceptre; then breaks into a surprising fit of pretend-tears, covering her face with her hands and peeping through to ascertain the effect of this changed tack.

'Come on, dear, do come in,' I say, and, climbing from the blanching sunlight to the cool shadowed interior, place one hand on her heaving back. She convulsively jerks the hand away.

Pretend-tears, yes, but even during this embarrassing carry-on, I recognise that the dry tears counterfeit the real tears sealed within the bunched back of the old woman in my care. Those tears she cannot afford to shed. She knows, and I know, and she knows I know, and I know she knows I know, that she is telling nothing but the truth when she claims I don't want her; and we both have to live with that. No wonder she weeps.

I falter.

'What shall we do?' I appeal to the ambulanceman, who must have amassed experience of comparable scenes on doorsteps and half way up stairs.

'Well, Mrs Cop,' he says, trying to get a purchase on May's conscience, 'we're all boiling and broiling out here. There's a heatwave, you know, and you're keeping us out in the mid-day sun.'

'Mad dogs and Englishmen!' sings May, and is on her feet before anyone's prepared for it. 'Go out in the mid-day sun!' she serenades us, as she is helped down the metal steps and walks, scornfully rejecting aid, then stumbling and snatching for it, up the path to our front door.

'I've had ot,' she informs me as she goes, leaving a murmur of neighbours to disperse into the shade of their separate dwellings, 'and I've been told you're to take me out with you wherever you go. I'm perfectly well able to visit places of interest and amusement, and you're not to keep me walled up in this ... Oh look, it's Brenda. *You* never came to see me,' she sulks, as I settle her in her special chair, and dispose of her luggage.

'I've not been out at all,' says Brenda.

'Well, and do you want me to feel sorry for you?' asks May irritably. '*I*'ve been in hospital, you might like to know – suffering.'

'Of course not,' Brenda replies. 'I was just explaining. Jess, I'm sorry but I think I need to . . .'

'So, what have you all been doing with yourselves?' May demands to know. 'I hope you've enjoyed your rest, Dee Dee – seven whole weeks to do nothing but enjoy yourself. A holiday-camp.'

'Jess,' says Brenda, tearfully. 'Please could you give me a hand? I need to . . .'

'Of course you don't,' punches May's voice, in ancient wrath of sibling-rivalry. 'It's my turn now.'

I assist Brenda to the loo, where she sits with wrinkled brow.

'It's quite . . . reposeful in here, isn't it?' she whispers, and the tension breaks. I crouch beside her, exchanging a pinched grin and a shrug of rue, our hands joined, and lay my head back against the wall. My eyes ramble the vitreous irregularities of the frosted pane behind her. Here we lurk, like twin apostates in a priest's hole, while May's presence registers as a devastating silence beyond the wall.

Nothing happens.

'Oh dear,' says Brenda. 'I feel I'm being listened to.'

'Tell you what,' I suggest. 'I'll go and put the radio on.'

With the tide of music comes my aunt's release from her immediate source of despair. I leave the music on to drown out the clock's ticking as we return to the living room to endure the wrath that is to come, as punishment for our abandonment.

May wonders why her question was not answered.

What question?

What we were doing with our rest-period. She believes it's called 'respite' now, isn't it, though why people living in the lap of luxury who don't have to go out to earn their crust should find themselves in need of respite escapes her. Now, in the hospital, nothing was too much trouble for the nurses... and she embarks on a detailed account of the qualities, habits, sayings, hairstyles, size, of the nurses, together with miscellaneous anecdotes concerning WRVS ladies and porters; holding us with hawk-eyes while she expounds this tale of fabulous dreariness to anyone not personally involved in the ward drama.

Having completed the account of the day-staff, she begins to fill us in on the night-nurses.

'Jessie,' says Brenda, 'do you think we ought to have something to eat. My tummy's rumbling. Is yours?'

'Shut up,' instructs May. 'I haven't finished yet.'

'Well, how about telling us the rest over a nice mug of soup?' I suggest. 'And I've bought in some of your favourite rolls, I can pop them in the oven, it won't take a moment.'

I struggle out of my inertia, semi-comatose with boredom, but conscious enough to know that I am, and have been, and will be on the rack. Even the dull kitchen seems a sanctuary from this oppression.

'*We* don't drink our soup from mugs,' May states, with contumely. '*We* have it in a dish, properly.'

'Well, that's fine; let's have it in a dish.'

'Oh, you do what you choose, don't let me try to impose my preferences on you. You two are dug in so nice and cosy here. Going off tittering in the toilet. Don't let me interfere with your ...'

I try a hug. The hug is flapped away as a dole which

May is too proud and clear-sighted to accept. She is in any case too morally bruised to allow herself to be touched.

'I was being nice to you, I was, before I fell down and broke my bone,' she complains. 'Anyway, it's too late now,' she tolls. 'What's done can't be changed. What have you been doing with yourself while I've been off there with those awful Welshwomen?'

She had taken against Mrs Jenkins as a moper and a talker, after a fortnight, and she didn't like the way she snored at night. This had had the effect for me of easing my laundry-load, for May withdrew my services, stating that her neighbour could do it if she had so much time on her hands to come in and gossip. May had begun to fret when Mrs Singh was released: for that quiet soul knew so little English, that she could be relied upon to agree smilingly with the most outrageous propositions May could think up to deposit in her ear. After Mrs Singh's disappearance, a further Welsh lady had appeared, on the western flank of May's bed. Sandwiched thus between foreigners, her high spirits had taken a tumble.

Apparently, the soup is too hot.

The soup in hospital was pleasantly tepid and didn't scald your tongue.

She used to like hot rolls but not any more. She accepts that if she leaves her soup and rolls for a few minutes, they will reach the desired temperature.

That Cheddar cheese she had in hospital was tasty: do I happen to have any in the fridge? – if so, she will have some, cut into square chunks. No, not that sort. Mild, she thought it was, or medium it might have been. No, not that shape. Oh come on, give it here, she will cut it herself if I am really so clueless.

For pudding, she will have apple tart and custard. Mind, the custard must not be too hot.

None in the house? Am I sure? Really, none? Blackberry? Goosegog? No tart of any description? She sinks her head back against the headrest, raising her eyes in disbelief to the ceiling; and all of a sudden, her eyelids droop: she topples into a heavy sleep, with a cascade of dishes from the tray on her lap, which I just manage to save.

Brenda and I look at one another, glazed, aghast.

'Would you very much mind, Jessie,' asks my aunt, 'if I just go upstairs and have a little nap myself – after all the ... excitement?'

She sails upstairs on the chair-lift and I pull the curtains. My head is being beaten from within by a hammer aiming at the inner membrane of my eyeball.

One does not think or feel anything under these circumstances: I'd forgotten that. There is just a minute-by-minute endurance of dulness and cacophony: the symphony that will be heard in Hell when we get into the auditorium there.

There she sleeps in her chair, and may go on waking and sleeping there for ten more years, fifteen.

She has put on weight since going into hospital and looks strong and hale. *Nothing wrong with her mind*, they were convinced. *Oh, she's such a sweet old lady – a real charmer*, they assured me at first. As time went on, the tune modulated. *Quite a character*, said the sister. Latterly, they began to look fazed, as if the staff had recognised the presence of a campaigning Vizigoth amid the peace-loving flock.

I can't stand it, I know I can't stand it. For however many more years. How did I ever stand it?

I was then in a state of grace and love.

The body in the chair emits a grunt; it jitters in its sleep and now is still.

What use is your life? I ask her silently.

To Brenda I phrase it ruefully thus: 'I think I've rather run out of oomph.'

'The first day back at school was always the worst,' she observes, with perfect comprehension. 'I remember being sure I couldn't stick it – I wrote a letter giving in notice at first break one autumn term but then I thought to myself: I'll just wait and see how I feel at the end of the week. And then I thought: only five weeks till half-term.'

'These things, my darling, are a parable,' I say, and the flowing-out of 'my darling' brings helpful tears to both our eyes.

'Oomph may revive over time,' she suggests; 'though I admit it has reached a lowish ebb.'

'I know I'm not perfect,' I plead with May. 'Very far from it – but please understand I'm doing my best.'

'Oh you and your Not Perfect. You're so selfish, you. Always thinking about how good you are, trying to cadge bonus points in God's book – never thinking about other people. In fact, of all the people I've ever met, Dee Dee, I think I'd have to say you were the most self-regarding.'

'If you say so, May. What can I bring you for your nightcap?'

May gives me her order but adds: 'I'm not going to bed yet, you fool.'

'But it's your time, love.'

'It *was* my time when I used to be in this prison before, but now I know different. I'd chat with the nurses all night if I wanted. *They* didn't mind. Said it was nice to have some intelligent conversation to while the night away.'

'But I need rest, May. I need it.'

'Oh – you. It's always me, me, me, isn't it, with you? Everything's too much trouble.'

'No, May,' I say with dead eyes. 'Not everything – just that I can't operate all the way round the clock: I have to have periods off duty. If you think about it, dear,' I try to remain temperate, to concentrate on stirring a heaped teaspoon of Horlicks into her mug of hot milk, 'the nurses have shifts, don't they, which keeps them fresh – whereas there's only the one of me and I can't keep going twenty-four hours round the clock. Can I? Much as I'd like to.'

'It's a matter of willingness, Dee Dee. The nurses are always willing to give me their time. They chat away – and brew up at all hours – and they're always laughing and joking. This drink's too hot,' she accuses, blowing on the steam with disgust. 'I keep telling you everything's too hot but you don't listen. You just don't listen. And anyway, I can't go to sleep, can I, in this heat. In the hospital we had fans brought to us on sticky nights like tonight – nice triangular fans, going round and round and round and ... you could watch them like a television ...'

Brennie retired to bed an hour and a half ago, at nine, dropping hefty hints to May that she should follow shortly. She lay uncomplainingly in the stifling heat, covered in a sheet, assuring me that her bladder was on top form, her eyes however measuring the distance between bed and commode with anxious calculation. When I came downstairs and suggested to May that she make tracks, she deigned no reply, casting an enquiring eye around the room, as if still in hope of sussing out sources of excitement in this monochrome post-hospital world.

'You must be so tired,' I urged.

'Speak for yourself.'

Now I wash up the Horlicks mug and move around conspicuously performing last-thing-at-night jobs: putting out the milk bottles, locking up, unplugging the television.

'Hoi!' she objects. 'I'm watching that!'

'No, you're not,' I riposte. 'We're going to bed.'

'I'm not.'

'Of course you are, May. We're all going up, the whole household's going to bed. Including May.'

'Mussolini,' she taunts me. 'Old Musso himself in person.'

'Please, May, let me help you upstairs to bed, love. You know it's time – and we need our beauty-sleep, don't we?' I wheedle.

'Leave me out of it. Go on, you go upstairs. Leave me down here all on my own-ee-oh to rot. Go on, bugger off, don't mind me.'

I sit down heavily on the settee. I take hold of the fat cushion and plump it on my knee. I take a deep breath, to remonstrate. But when I look up, I see a terrible triumph on Jacob's mother's face; she is actually laughing at me, although (it's odd) her mouth is not smiling; on the contrary, her jaw is set fast, bulging out. But I know she's scoffing, sneering.

The use of the cushion . . .

I stare at my fingers gripping into its spongy viscera.

Not for throwing . . . for other uses . . . shut her up . . . it would shut her up . . .

I place the cushion neatly, fastidiously, just so, at the far end of the settee.

'Come on, May,' I say, holding out a hand to her. The

hand is friendly, stretched out in invitation; the hand is not a fist. 'Up you come, silly.'

'You're treating me like a baby.'

'You're behaving like one.'

'Oh, am I, I wonder why.' She speculates on the possible reasons why anyone should behave in a childish manner in the presence of Jesus Wept. She goes on to conjecture as to why my husband, her son, should have found it intolerable to go on living with a woman whose idea of love is to sit on you with her big fat bum, singing hymns and psalms . . .

'Well then,' I interrupt, 'I'll just have to go to bed without you, and I'm afraid you'll be left down here on your own all night.'

Magazine articles advise mothers of difficult children to take this line of handing over responsibility for herself to the tantrum-thrower.

'Oh, you do that, go on, do that, see if I care,' May storms. 'But I tell you what I'll do, I'll shit and piss and shit and piss all over the floor and when you get downstairs in the morning you'll find your precious tidy house is a sewer . . .'

I believe her.

I stand suspended, by the open door.

There is a small defect on the wall, where a photograph of Jacob and Nella used to hang; the picture of the two of them at the hill fort on Caer Caradoc, shot just before Nella took the short cut down the north slope by sliding down on her bottom, shouting 'Ouch! Ouch!' because there were hidden stones in the turf. But where this picture used to hang, there is a tiny hole, which at some future date must be painted over. It is not so large as to require plastering with filler, but some step will have to be taken.

'Piss and shit and shit and piss . . .' May continues to

194

chant, until the words pass from threat to credo, from credo to meaningless mantra with which she anaesthetises her mind.

Then she pauses, to give a wide yawn and a belch.

And is off again, far louder: 'Shitty shitty shitty pity . . .'

Precisely what happened then is not clear. I know the noise was terrible, blood-curdling. There was some sort of skirmish. Some violent conundrum failed to be solved.

I was pouring blood from my nose and she was lying in silence face-downwards on the mat.

She was not bleeding. The noise had stopped.

'It's ridiculous,' says Peter Fox to the policewoman. 'Utterly ridiculous and preposterous. She would never, never have . . . Jessie is just incapable of . . .'

'No, Peter,' I correct him. 'I'm not. I'm not incapable.'

'Look here,' says Peter, 'would you please realise who this woman is. This,' he said, and waves his arms around, out of synchronisation with one another, 'is Jessie Copplestone. *Jessie*.' As if this explained everything.

'What's happened?' Jacob rushes in to Casualty. 'What's going on?'

'How does that concern you?' asks Peter heatedly. Jacob stares with some surprise: the mother's boy has turned on the ladies' man.

'She's my mother,' he replies mildly.

Peter snorts contemptuously but addresses no further words to him. He goes on explaining to the policeman that, due to my upset state of mind, nothing I am accusing myself of should be taken seriously.

A nurse and a white-coated woman squeak in to the side-ward, wheeling a metal and glass machine.

'How is she?' asks Jacob. 'What happened?'

From the side-ward comes a thin, wailing chant: 'Shitty shitty shitty pity . . .'

'Oh my God,' groans Jacob. 'What's going on?'

Catherine arrives headlong, wearing a raincoat over her nightdress.

'Cathy,' I say. 'I think I . . .'

'No, she didn't,' cuts in Peter. He puts an arm across my chest, between me and Cathy. 'She didn't do anything of the sort. She wouldn't and she couldn't.'

'Peter,' I say. 'I could.'

'Could fucking what?' demands Jacob.

'There was some sort of . . . fight,' I say. 'I must have started it. I must have struck her. Would you please,' I beg the policeman, 'take a statement? I want to make a statement.'

Cathy takes the policeman on one side. I hear her murmuring to him but cannot make out the words. Peter has now planted his large body between me and my husband. Jacob takes no notice. He vigorously rubs his unshaven face with both palms, so that I hear the rasp of the abrading bristles.

Then he nabs a passing doctor.

'Comfortable . . . investigations . . . taken a fall,' is all I hear.

'Not *again*,' says Jacob.

'She didn't take a fall,' I say. 'I pushed her . . . I think.'

'You pushed her? What do you mean, you pushed her?' A scared look comes over his face, he takes a step backwards.

'Shut up, Jessie. Of course you didn't,' says Peter.

'I did – at least I felt as if I did.'

'Jessie, will you shut up?'

'Why do you keep telling my wife to shut up?' demands Jacob. 'Get out from between us.'

'Your *wife*? ... *Your* wife?'

'Look, you bloody parrot, flap off and perch some-where else or I will pick you up and move you myself.'

'Leave her alone, you bastard,' says Cathy. And runs at Jacob from one side, so that he cannons off-balance into the coffee machine. 'And leave him alone. It's totally your fault, you bastard, you bastard, you ought to be ...'

'Cathy,' I say. 'Please ...'

'Now then, no need to get upset,' says the policeman. 'No need for pushing people around, Mrs ...'

'Ms,' says Cathy. She is red-faced, breathing hard, and can be heard saying, 'I'd like to kick you where it hurts ...'

'Ms ... what did you say your name was, madam, Ms?'

'Catherine Davies.'

'Cathy, that's your maiden name,' I say.

'So?'

'Now now,' says the policeman. 'Now now,' and looks round for the woman constable, who has vanished into the nurses' room, where a doctor is examining X-rays of May's head and limbs.

'And don't you call me a parrot,' says Peter to Jacob, highly wrought, having sat on this indignity for several minutes. 'Though to be honest I'd rather be a parrot than a swine.'

'Did you hit your mother-in-law, Mrs Copplestone?' asks the policewoman.

'Yes,' I say. 'I do think I did. We hit each other. Definitely. But I had been wanting to kill her.'

There is a tense silence.

'Definitely,' I say. 'Why don't you write it down?'

Cathy comes up close, our eyes are on a level, and

she takes both my hands in hers. 'Are you sure, love?' she asks.

'I think so.'

'She can't have . . .' Peter begins.

'If you insist on saying that again, I shall scream,' says Cathy, 'and I really mean it.'

'Will you shush? for heaven's sake,' says an icy male voice. 'This is a hospital.'

'I want you to charge me,' I tell the policeman. 'And I want to plead guilty. Now.'

The policeman will just have a word with the patient and the hospital staff, if I will wait in this room. On my own, if no one minds.

Incontinence pads and kidney bowls are stacked on shelves; surgical gloves, like the spectres of skins stripped wholesale from hands, slither off a pile. They have put me in a cupboard. There is nowhere to sit. In that peculiar metallic light out there, Jacob looked tarnished. Both of us are blighted humans. Ashen, I stand in shadowless fluorescence, my head against a filing cabinet. The sense of my own darkness spreads internally, like the knowledge of incurable disease when it has once been diagnosed.

They scoop me out of that box.

They smile as they usher me into this office, handing me this cup of tea in a chipped green cup, which I now raise to my lips as instructed.

Figures of uniformed foreigners in a world of estrangement: my eyes slip past one face to the next, not registering more than a blur of features, a blondness, a tallness.

'Well,' says the policeman. 'I've spoken to Mrs Copplestone, and a doctor has been through the X-rays with me. The lady was quite insistent that you did attack her.'

'What does she say I did?' I ask tonelessly.

'That you attacked her from behind with a poker, red-hot from the fire, and smashed her about the head twenty or thirty times. Then she alleges you punched her in the stomach, and set her dress alight. She says she's always been secretly frightened of your history of violent rages.'

'So . . . are you going to charge me?'

'Mrs Copplestone, do you have an open fire?'

'No.'

'Or a poker?'

'No.'

'And the elder Mrs Copplestone has no bruising except on the top of her arm. The thigh-bone looks to be fractured but that may apparently be an old injury. The story seems a confused sort of nightmare . . . what needs to be explained is the bruising on the arm. Can you shed light on that?'

'I grabbed her.'

'To hold her up or push her down?'

The question seems so meaningless. I know my desire was a violent one. As on so many occasions, a phantom arm has risen and struck, and struck again, that piteous being. Many times my ghost rose, loomed, towered above her; my hands clenched with will to wring or smother. I try to put it all in sequence.

'She wouldn't go to bed. She was shouting. I lost my temper, I was in a frenzy, I dashed at her and grabbed her arm, and sort of shook it up and down. She screamed and flailed her arms about, and lashed out so that she punched me on the nose. I screamed. We both roared at the tops of our voices. I kept on screaming and screaming at her. But it was not words, it was just roaring. I wanted to kill her, I've felt that ... danger in me, for months. We both lost balance, she fell partly on me and partly on the floor, and then there was no more noise. I thought she was dead.'

There is a stain on the skirt of the white coat of the doctor standing nearest to me, on a level with my eyes. It could well be blood, though it might also be gravy or just miscellaneous dirt. I study the dimensions of this stain. Millions of germs could be spawning on that pure coat, they could spread over a whole hospital: should I mention it to her?

Can the germs be stopped from spreading in any case?

Is it best just to go on pretending one hasn't seen?

Necrotising fasciitis is the phrase that triggers in my mind. I don't know if they've ever had a case at Copthorne.

'Your friends tell me you're under a great deal of stress. May I suggest you go home and get some rest? If it is felt that further investigations are called for, we'll be in touch.'

Nobody would charge me with anything. There was no atonement. I came home here to an empty house, Jane Venner having taken Brenda home with her. At first Cathy wouldn't leave me. She was sticking to me like a leech, she said; not letting me out of her sight. It didn't matter about the baby, she added; she'd expressed some milk, it was in the fridge and Alan could do the feed from a bottle.

'I did want to hit her,' I said. I'd been saying it over and over again, to anyone who would listen.

'You probably did,' she says. 'And you might perhaps have grabbed her roughly. But it can't have been very hard, can it? She's on top form.'

'It felt hard.'

'I'd have murdered her years ago,' says Cathy, matter-of-factly. I don't know what right I have to be shocked by anything other people say: perhaps it's force of habit, but this casualness jars inexpressibly.

'Would you mind going now, Cathy? I need to be on my own.'

She'd rather not leave me on my own; thinks I'll do myself some harm. She says I'm off-balance. I open the door and show her out into the dark.

Here I am, wandering the house, self-accompanied, self-estranged. I view where it happened, the spinning out-of-control; I look into May's Mayless bedroom, where a pair of beige carpet slippers peeps out from under her pale blue quilted dressing-gown left dangling on a peg. The shabby slippers hold the shape of her feet, wide and trodden at the heel; the dressing-gown is elbowed and seated.

The thing is, I did love her.

That's the odd thing. I did. The bulk of her, the blare of her, the blue eyes of her, that brought Jacob to mind whenever they met my wooings. The fact that she had stood out to be who she is; and will do, to the end of her time.

So I did care for you, May. I did not not care.

That is surely something: I plead with the blue quilted dressing-gown.

I remember how scared her eyes could be; timid behind the bawling, brawling voice.

And you were old. You were needy and insecure. You needed above all the life-guaranteeing love of a person you could trust: and that was me. I took that on.

So I did not not care.

But I could hate you. For you were without mercy. Always testing, wearing me out and tearing me up. Tying me down, keeping me in.

Is that an excuse?

I hated you.

Hated myself for hating you.

Because I loved you.

Ill logic maybe it is; but heart's truth. I sit now on your vacated bed, and the blue quilted dressing-gown, with its smell of staleness and baby powder dangles at me like a hung May. Nobody has pulled the curtains against the evil of the darkness out there, with its many reflections of a shame-ravaged face adrift in here.

Several hours escaped me.

Now, more crouched than curled in bed in the spare room, I am overwhelmed by their speaking absences, those beloved faces that met my needs as I met theirs: healing what had been broken in me since God-knows-when, with their gratitude, their preference for the word 'Jess' above all other names in the world.

Black and curdled, my mind forges excuses and flings accusations in the same breath. *You turned against a helpless old woman. You took out your own sense of rejection on her. No one will respect you now.*

I couldn't ask her to come back. She'd goad and hector and rant until I did it again, or worse. Anyhow they wouldn't let her come back to the care of a person who might harm her.

And, under sick layers of guilt, there is an explosion of relief.

She won't come back.

CHAPTER 13

Late the following evening he came to me; he let himself in with his own key, which he laid on the morning-room table.

'I'll leave that there for you, Jessie dear,' he said, in his beautiful voice, that will always seem reliable however many lies it has told. 'I should have returned it yonks ago. I hope you don't mind my coming in – this last time. I saw your light was on.'

'No . . . no.' I had been expecting him. Can spirits catch faint echoes of strayed others turning to them before turning finally away? I'd dreamed my bed was pitching from side to side, great shuddering rockings in the hot, damp night; and then I dreamed that I was awake and still it bucked beneath me. I stumbled out. My nightgown was soaked with sweat, in the breathless night. The window was wide open but the air was static. Downstairs it was fresher. Then I heard him enter the house. I thought, *Oh yes, it's Jacob come home*.

He aligned the Yale key between the edge of the table and a scratch on the surface.

'How are you, Jess?' he asked, in a thoroughly normal voice.

'To tell you the truth: dark. I'm in the dark. I feel my own . . . blackness. I'm finding it hard to live with that. And alone. That too. But I'll be all right.'

'I've acted like a swine. None of it's your fault.'

I'll have to change that forty watt bulb, I thought; one can hardly see in this room. The light dimmed and diminished us both (I saw myself in the mirror, sallow, shabby) to common unloveliness. And he is a handsome man, but in this light appeared dull and greasy-skinned.

'It can't have been right between us or else you'd never have gone,' I said. 'You *couldn't* have gone if it had been right. Could you?'

'Aren't you angry?'

'Often. Yes, often I am.'

'At the moment?'

'No.' I shook my head, quivering with tired tenderness for the husband whose likeness he bore. 'Not now with you in the room and speaking to me as if I were a human being. You see, Jacob, you were quite simply my life. You were – where I lived and moved and had my being. I've got to, somehow, take myself back.'

He sat down at the table, still fiddling with the key; lost for words. I suddenly saw him for what he is – a rather uncomplicated, easy-going, healthy, virile, good-looking chap who'd got himself married to a woman of consuming religious passion. My intense and devout practice of the pieties of normal life must have been a strain. A ghastly meaningfulness must have burdened every simple act. The saying of grace, the God bless at night. My soulful translations of his sexual loving into mystical raptures ... how my consciousness must have oppressed him when he was just trying to let go; have a good time.

'I know I must let you go,' I acknowledged. 'We were mismatched, ill-mated. At least from your point of view.'

Jacob, my Jacob, reached out a hand and grasped my wrist.

'I'd come back tomorrow – this moment – if it weren't for the baby. Honest-to-God I would, honestly.'

Oh: come. Oh Jacob, come. Part of me breathed that prayer.

The other part said, jadedly, Come come, Jacob; saw my past darling in a God-forsaken light, as a shadowed someone whose good-natured sturdiness I'd never trust again. I'd been so boundlessly confident of him and have been (anger stirs) contemptuously handled …

… handled. The hands of someone you love, stretched forth appeasingly, with their life-lines and character-lines, teasing the mind with forked pathways, each an eventual cul de sac – hands are personal and intimate as faces. My body stroked and cradled in those hands; those hands that cradle and stroke her body. But out of hers he has conjured a life-changing child.

'Your teeth need checking,' I said. 'You missed your last appointment.'

'Yes, yes, I'd better see about that.'

He won't. But he has good teeth; they don't seem to rot at the same rate as other people's, even though he smokes and is slapdash about plaque. He'd ignore the dental floss I bought for him. Anyhow they are stained with tar and need polishing.

'Also you'll need to get May fixed up somewhere,' I reminded him, 'Had you thought of a place like Leagrove House on Hereford Road? It's one of these Abbeyfields set-ups – been going ten years – and residents have self-contained bedsits but they're attended by volunteer carers. The only thing is, I expect there's a waiting list a mile long.'

'Don't worry,' Jacob said, quietly, copingly. 'I'll sort that out. Anyone would have snapped, Jessie, under the pressure I put you under.'

'Well, never mind about that,' I came in, just as

abruptly. 'I can't undo it.' My whole future stretches ahead as a space for coming to terms with the fact that I, the wayfaring Christian, became an abuser. That *is* the ugly word: abuser. 'The trouble with this heat,' I say, 'is that it makes one so sluggish. I know I ought to clean up in here – look at the mess – but I can't bring myself to start. In fact, when things deteriorate to a certain state, you don't know *where* to start.'

A layer of dust coats the piano I've left unplayed for years but kept polished to glossy perfection. Yesterday I opened the lid and let my fingers stumble through some girlhood piece: I had to stop after a while, I'd set up such a roar in the untuned body of the instrument, a jangling vibration booming round and round, like the echo of some affliction at once deadly and ridiculous. And after my fingers were removed, the stunned wood continued to echo with the din. When it had faded, I laid my ear to the case and caught a thin, tinny vibration which did not seem to want to die.

'Jessie – oh, I . . .' you began, and I waited, but you could not think of anything to say. Your tongue was lame; flopping impotently. It had always been my mistake to expect you to speak in words; there are other languages, I see that now, and I might have learned them, such as this of the body, which I long to speak, but have left it too late. As you wrapped your arms around me, I reached mine round you and smelt your intimate smell, so lovely, of spice and sweat, wood-shavings, tobacco, and also the suspicion of someone else's musky perfume caught in the fibres of your sweater.

'I'll let you go,' I said.

CHAPTER 14

'In my opinion,' says Brenda, 'and speaking, you under-
stand, as a geologist and not as a reader of the Book of
Revelation, it's the beginning of the End of the World.
And only ourselves to blame.'

Autumn leaves are drifting on the pathway in waves
of scarlet, tawny and rust; they poured from the trees
as I turned my key in the lock, to find the morning
room crammed with two tribes of visitors, the sacred
and the profane, conversing in the dialects of Babel.

'Ah! here she is! the wanderer returns!' cries Brenda's
friend Tisha, no doubt relieved to give place to a
mediator so experienced in these religious wars. Tisha
stands with Brenda for Geography and Science, against
the Apocalypse as expounded by Deborah Pym and a
trinity of disciples, who are all smiling dreadfully in
a row on the settee. Behind my bowl of golden chrysanthemums Deborah is biting into a slice of lemon cake.
Behind Deborah's back, through the picture window,
the limes on the far shore have turned ginger and ochre.
Crumbs powder Deborah's upper lip as she greets me:

'We were just discussing the End of the World,' she
fills me in.

'Have some lemon cake, dear,' says Peter, bustling; he
organises me a cup of tea and ushers me fussily into his
vacated seat. 'Baked it myself, of course, and brought it

round for you and dear Brenda ... but I'm afraid we've made some inroads already. Come on, sit you down, after all you're a Worker now.'

'Isn't Ben with you?' I ask Deborah, accepting the cup with a smile, looking round for him.

'Didn't you know?' enquires Deborah, dark eyes wide, face plunged forward almost into the chrysanthemums.

'Know what?'

'He's gone.'

'Gone ... where?'

'Christian Science,' says Deborah, nodding her head and then shaking it, relishing her outrage, sucking all the juice out of those (to her) wicked syllables. 'At Greyfriars. It sears my heart,' she adds, 'to think that the lamb has escaped the fold and taken itself off to the butcher's slab. What can I say?'

'Oh ... ah.' I raise my eyebrows in a weary feint at proper shock. It's my first half-day at the Library, and I could have done without the welcoming party of highly strung Jeremiahs. The church has not seen me over the summer, and I murmur an inward prayer that our zealous friend won't find herself detouring to the subject of backsliding daughters.

'I take it as a sign,' Deborah informs us all.

'Of?'

'These Latter Days.'

Peter coughs into his plump hand in response to my pleading look. He leads off into the weather, that reliable stand-by, taking it as axiomatic that this cannot be considered inflammatory.

He mentions that it is exceptionally warm for the time of year. His garden is still (or should he say 'again'?) in flower. Myriad shoots shooting and blooms blossoming. His Choisya Ternata, for instance, the spring plant he's so fond of, has already come into flower. What a bonus! Would we credit it?

Brenda, whose drift into the tranquil beyond of Zen has been stemmed with the departure of Averil for a new job in Wolverhampton, has revived with the colourful autumn into a late burst of environmental commitment. She has shuffled all her memberships, renewing some, cancelling others, calculating the financial possibilities of new subscriptions. 'This is just what I was trying to *say*. We are seeing the first effects of Global Warming. Spring in autumn. Summer going on past its time and next spring here before its time. It's not bonus, Peter, it's blight!'

'Oh dear,' says Peter inadequately.

Mrs Thrower from the Percy Thrower Garden Centre has stated that the scorching summer has killed conifers and mature trees all round the area. And Bayley's Garden Centre has said that though our lawns seem green again, they are actually dying underneath.

Nature is doomed, Brenda informs Deborah Pym across the chrysanthemums. By our car-emissions.

'Armageddon,' says Miss Pym, in an I-told-you-so voice. She explains that the car-exhausts are the fumes of Satan and that my aunt is muddling the instrument with the first cause.

'Glory be,' Brenda moans.

Deborah chimes in by seconding that, and going on to speak in more detail of the Glory of the Divine Scheme; and I know, *I know*, that at any moment, she'll cry *Selah*! and that Brenda will enquire mildly but pointedly as to whether Miss Pym has yet converted to unleaded petrol?

'Yes,' I say to Peter, 'it is uncommonly warm.'

'Quite pleasant though,' he responds.

'I couldn't stand that burning fiery furnace, could you?' asks Tisha.

'Yet, isn't it odd, you can hardly remember it when it's over, can you?' asks Peter. 'Extreme heat and cold – a bit like pain and pleasure – you remember that they happened but what they felt like – you lose completely.'

All summer our lawns burned and browned; by September they were baked hard. I'd pad out into the shock of heat carrying bowls scooped from my used bathwater, to fling on the flower-beds; and the water would stand for a while, gleaming on the crusted surface, unable to seep down. But while some plants withered, others throve, efflorescing in tropical luxuriance. Stepping out morning by morning was like a quantum visit to Texas or Mexico, into a bath of densely scalding heat. Through the phases of my bereavement, the drought deepened, in violent light that allowed retreat behind ultra-violet protective sunglasses, a hide-away where no one could see I'd been crying.

Hazel and her almost-husband pushed their newborn baby through the Quarry. Their arms were as sunburnt as if they'd summered in Tenerife and, with the fair-haired children who galloped out of the Swimming Baths towards them, they resembled a Nordic family, lustrous with outdoor health.

'This is Sebastian,' said Hazel shyly, unable quite to meet my eyes.

Jacob's son lay sleeping under the shadow of a tasseled sunshade, in a shining chromium buggy. Curled up he lay, such a tiny being, but robust, with bare, plump arms and legs; I bent my head, tears filming my eyes. The silken tassels brushed my bare shoulder, soft and cool.

'What a lovely name. What a dear ... mite,' I said, straightening up, dragging my gaze away.

It was good, I thought. It was good that he'd arrived

at last, neutralising many of the pangs that had been conceived of his unreality. Solid and strong he lay there, with his dark thatch: like a statement that was out in the open. His lax mouth quivered as he slept. His tiny hands were closed, the soles of his feet puckered as if from the sea. Here, instead of a nightmare, was Sebastian.

I looked out over the parched grass, longing for rain. The river level was right down.

'He's dark though; not fair like the rest of you.'

'Oh, that's just baby-hair,' said Hazel. 'It will all fall out most probably, and he'll be bald as a coot. Lara's did.'

Lara and Fergus were creating, to go and bounce on the suspension bridge, to make the old ladies sea-sick, they said.

'Delightful kids,' observed Hazel wryly.

It had been kind of her to show me the baby; so I said and so I meant. She could have hurried by. But she chose to believe that I had renounced all claim to her almost-husband and her brood. It was kind.

Jacob sustained, for my benefit, a foolish but well-meaning pretence of having none but the remotest acquaintance with his son: neither mentioning nor casting his eyes down to the beloved child while I was there. He said business was good but it was pure hell working outdoors in this heat. He hoped for a spot of rain. They were renting in Meole Brace, waiting for me and Brenda to sell up, when they'll buy a larger place of their own, and we'll buy a smaller one. It was thoughtful of him to pretend, but quite unnecessary.

I did not linger very long; but just before we passed out of range, his eyes slewed towards me, I caught and became entangled in a look that made me gasp. For it left me, after we disengaged, with the name: Nella. Yes,

Nella. He was surely, without any doubt, Nella's father. I let myself know that consciously for the first time.

Parched patches of the Quarry grass quivered in the heat. Dust or pollen in the air troubled my eyes and throat; light needled from the river.

Everything blanched. Two paces into the whitened world, a collapse began.

I took out my inhaler methodically. Two puffs; okay; walked on, up through the blue gates into the stony shade behind Chad's. My feet crunched round the gravel path amongst the city of lichened tombs, amongst the darkness of the yews and holly. I was glad I'd seen.

For Nella was mine. Mine just as much as she could be anyone's. My daughter with Jacob. And my love for Nella was boundless, so universal that it eclipsed the little globe of love I'd felt for Jacob: though that had filled both eye and heart and hands, and would have been enough for a lifetime.

Apparently I was raving when I came home. Brenda in alarm suggested she call a doctor.

Then I came out of it; I said 'Really, Brennie, I'm quite all right. I'm perfectly normal.'

'Oh, you did give me a turn,' she fussed.

'Sorry,' I said. But I was glad I saw.

'I thought you'd had a religious vision,' she said. 'Going on like that about the firmament and the waters under the firmament. Good grief.'

'No, just an asthma attack. Made me a bit weird in the head.'

It was disgraceful, said Brenda, how practically every household in Shrewsbury had someone with asthma. It never used to be like this. The Council should be made to sit down in the middle of Castle Foregate and breathe in those ruddy fumes for a day. Then we'd see.

Since May's departure, Brenda has become notably

more militant, as if a long-coveted space had been made available.

Now she says to Peter, 'Never mind your Choisya Ternata, Peter, what about the Crassula Helmsii? – what about that?'

'Never heard of him.'

A foreign weed, apparently, a noxious alien species, has found its way into aquatic areas of Shropshire, where it is destroying rare plants. According to Brenda, this Swamp Stonecrop has reached Bomere and Brown Moss at Whitchurch, where it is wreaking havoc. Men with black plastic bags are understood to be patrolling these areas, capturing it.

Tisha agrees that everything is going from bad to worse. She instances the statue of Sabrina in the Dingle, whose face vandals have smashed off (but Deborah maintains that Sabrina had it coming, being a profane idol and a mermaid); and Hercules has graffiti over him (an even worse abomination, that Hercules with his club, Deborah urges, so vehemently that one could almost suspect her of having attacked these civic treasures herself). *And*, Tisha notifies us, there was a *vile object* on the Angel St Michael's hand at the War Memorial. She saw it herself.

'What sort of vile object?' enquires Evie from the couch.

'Nothing I could name in polite company,' Tisha replies coyly. But it just goes to show how the world is going downhill.

'Is it still there?' asks Evie, her imagination evidently aroused.

'I've no idea,' says Tisha. She is avoiding St Michael on her outings.

'Youth today' is anathematised.

Tisha changes the subject. She is a member of the

Little Wenlock Women's Institute, and describes a most fascinating talk they lately enjoyed on modelling in beeswax. The speaker had brought along with her some of her prize works, including a dinosaur, a squirrel, owls, and Brother Cadfael sitting at a table.

'You ought to join, Jessie,' Tisha urges, 'we get some scrumptious spreads of chutney and banana loaf. And some jolly intelligent discussion.'

'Well, I'm out to work now, Tisha, don't forget. Much as I'd like to.'

Being back at the Library draws the scattered fragments of myself back together again; I roam the bookshelves where my earliest adult self, Jessie Parry, began her working life. But now of course we are computerised: although that had come in before I left, I've had to be 'reskilled' as they call it. Beneath the statue of Darwin, greenly tarnished, looking so bourgeois and respectable on his chair, with *The Origin of Species* open on his knee, I dawdled, having arrived far too early; and looked up at his crossed trousered knees, his left boot in the air, its sole above my face, his bushy eyebrows in sculpted silhouette against the sky: who could have known from that smug bronze icon of Shrewsbury respectability the dynamite of his mind? Broad and Sons, Founders, London, had cast him. The Shropshire Horticultural Society had erected him in 1897. I perched on one of the benches, my eyes vaguely mulling over the lie he had become: a cosy gent, bookish, benign, eminent Old Boy of Shrewsbury School. Safely dead.

You, I thought, *closed the churches. You predicted me.* I'd been superseded, by a fitter, more fertile specimen. May too had been discarded. Nature abhors the barren, the past-it. She'd put up a hell of a fight though. And we'd both survived.

At Haughmond there is a farmworker's cottage,

which had fallen into disuse and been condemned as unfit for human habitation. There was even a tree growing up through the roof. It's been restored now, and has won some sort of restoration design award. I liked the way the tree found lodging there; its sapling sheltered until it burst through the remains of the roof, staggering passers-by. There was a toughness there, a sign, and not of Last Things, although of course they've got rid of it now.

'And how is dear May?' asks Deborah, as she and her disciples get up, preparatory to departure. Ladies' fingers insert themselves into gloves; the gloves reach for the handles of venerable navy handbags.

'Yes, she's settled in pretty well,' I answer, after fractional hesitation. She enjoys my visits, which license a spectacular drama, involving cowering in her chair and crying out in a loud voice 'Don't hit me! Don't hit me!', explaining that she's only a poor old woman, whose purse and Post Office book I am welcome to steal; as long as I won't tie her to the bedstead and beat her with a steak-tenderiser.

'If you'd like me to go away, of course I will,' I say gently. 'I don't want to upset you, I just came to see how you were getting on.'

'Certainly not,' she says, scandalised. 'You've only just come. At 1400 hours precisely.'

I sit at a safe distance: safe for her, safe for me. Yet I know she aches for touch. I could offer it; but wouldn't her bruised mind flinch from the outstretched arm, whose gesture might awaken a nightmare of double meaning, threatening what security she's achieved? I carry my guilt more calmly now, balancing it carefully, not denying the reality of the burden but aware that I must live with the flawed woman I've discovered myself to be. I bag the stuff up and hope it will die off, like Brenda's Crassula Helmsii.

I tried to explain my feelings but May answered, brusquely, 'Bullshit.'

Since she's been at The Bower, she has been calling me Jessie. I asked her why she'd always previously called me Dee Dee?

'Don't you know?' she asked, surprised.

'No, I never have.'

'It was short for "The Daughter", that's why. "The D", you see – hence, "Dee Dee".'

'Oh – right. I see.' As I wandered home after a punishing three hours, my exhausted brain kept turning this explanation over, holding it to the light, this way and that. It was the day after the first downpour which marked the end of the drought. Cloud-reflecting drops still hung from the tips of leaves, their greenness washed fresh of weeks of dust.

'Dee Dee', I thought, signalled May's appropriation of me as the daughter she'd coveted. I belonged to her and for her and with her. Yet at the same time, it suggested the tenuousness of her hold, a code-name she'd secretly baptised me with, to tie me to the duties and obligations of a daughter.

Now that Dee Dee was dead, never to be resurrected, I was turned loose to be Jessie, whoever she might be, a fact that May seemed to have conceded by ceasing to tweak the tether of the nickname. Yet so often she had called me 'mum' and insisted on her own daughterhood. Her great beak open and snapping at my fingers as they offered tidbits to appease her angry hunger, she had thrashed her flightless wings in my face. All that outcry claimed a mother's authority, a child's dependence. It was a conundrum I could never quite focus, and yet I comprehended it, from within my own cavernous neediness.

'Yes, May is holding her own,' I assure Deborah. 'Actually I think she is really being courageous. It can't be easy.'

'I thought I might pay her a little visit,' suggests Deborah, innocent of the pillows and execrations that would bombard her as soon as she got her nose in the door.

'Oh – maybe wait a while, Deborah, until she's got her bearings a bit more,' I suggest hastily.

'So are you going to the demo in the Square, to protest about the welfare cuts?' asks Peter.

'Certainly,' I answer. 'With Cathy. Are you?'

'If you are.'

The fond look he beams upon me does not pass unnoticed amongst the guests. For I am a free and single woman now, which no one here can countenance as other than transitional, so deeply inwoven do I seem with utility in the fabric of family. It is felt that I should be recycled and put to new use; so valuable a resource should surely not be wasted. Granted, a plump woman of my age, with poor skin, is not likely at such a late hour to snare a new husband. But Peter, epicene, shrinking, has a paradoxical eligibility: a motherly woman such as I seem to be would not threaten.

'See you there then,' he promises.

I wrote again to Shirehall about Nella, asking if they could try again to forward a letter to her old address.

My heart beats high as I sit by the window reading Mrs Jones' answer. She reminds me that the natural mother was antagonistic to me, and there is no reason to suppose that her feeling will have altered, though she moots the possibility that (now that Eleanor is of age), the young woman may have left home, and that her mother may be less unwilling to forward a letter from me.

The leaves corrode and decay, crumbling as I rake them off the lawn. The dye of autumn has reached that stage at which the season seems to sicken. A crimson rash speckles the russet leaves I brush up, and the yellowish-green remnant on the bushes of a lower terrace of the garden has a bilious hue in the forensic sunlight. Corrosion is everywhere, forcing one to acknowledge what had always been evident: that the season's splendour was always a distillation of poison, spreading through the tree's system as the year's sap fails. Livid stains disease my eye; and the stricken limes across the river, still in themselves making a beautiful and impressive statement, are prejudiced with the rest in my general jaundice.

The heap is now a mound, a tumulus, half as high as I am. I keep on raking and brushing, until much of the detritus is gathered in.

'Don't forget to hunt for hedgehogs before you burn that lot, will you, dear?' asks my aunt anxiously, as she registers the dimensions of the pile. 'That would be an inviting den to some little beastie.'

Really I should not burn it at all but bag it for leaf-mould. But I shall burn it as a pyre.

By spring we may be out of here. Viewers come and go, and *Oh! what a simply lovely place!* they croon. *Why are you leaving?*

It's far too big for my aunt and me.

This seems to satisfy them. Strangers' fingers prowl the carved banister and, wrenching open a cupboard to get an intimate view into the airing cupboard, one viewer was at once embarrassed and triumphant to find that the knob came away in his hand.

There the bald man stood with the knob, saying, 'This came off. Sorry about that.'

Jacob should have seen to that knob, and countless other bits and bobs that were constantly falling off.

'Needs a bit doing to it,' said Mr Rhys, pursuing his advantage.

'Well, only superficially,' I insisted, bridling. 'The structure's fundamentally sound. My parents owned the house before me: my family has lived here for eighty-odd years.'

How this might prove to our prospective buyer that the house was architecturally sound eludes me now: but it made a sort of sense to me.

'We'd have a full structural survey done, naturally,' said Mr Rhys, sensibly reserving judgement. Between finger and thumb, he offered me the knob, which I accepted and promptly stuck back into its hole. 'We do like the view,' he said, pulling aside the net curtain to reveal the river in one of its smooth, dark-olive moods, bearing the brilliant whiteness of a fleet of swans. 'It's a feature,' he observed. 'A definite Feature. A vista. A prospect.'

Come and view my newly-acquired slice of river, he'd advertise his property to his friends. I shivered at the thought of the house surviving without us.

'You'll miss such a lovely home – especially as your family has been here so long,' nattered his wife at the front door.

'Yes and no,' I said. Rather, I thought, no and yes. We look forward to our flat, free of the mahogany heaviness of Edwardian furniture: I crave whiteness; pale walls which I will paint myself; white bookshelves and desk, where I imagine myself enjoying first secret go at a loot of Library acquisitions. After this interior, so darkly brooding with the shadows of memories, I need a plainer-dealing light.

In the event, the Rhyses have backed out. A young Mr Howdle from Harthill, a watercolour artist, is taking the house, and as he is a first-time buyer, the transaction looks fair to be quick and painless. Intuitive fellow-feeling makes it easier to relinquish the house to him.

Having sifted for hedgehogs, I burned the leaves. They buckled and crinkled in the heat, then crackled up into a short-lived blaze, with that melancholy, kindling scent.

Perhaps I ought not to trouble Nella, I thought, standing aside, with scorched face, in my jeans and wellingtons.

Leave her be, I told myself.

> But I'd not be meddling with Nella.
> I love her, wish her well.
> How can it hurt Nella to know someone still has her at heart through all these years?
> How could that be construed as selfishness?

Leave her be.

She is her own person.

She'd come looking for you if she needed to.

You might pass on your damage.

> But Nella might have thought all along I'd abandoned her.
> I could reassure her.
> I could say, it wasn't as you thought, not at all.
> I'd see her darling eyes.

You'd see Jacob's darling eyes.

It's just another way of trying to repossess him.

It's your need you're answering, not Nella's.
Nella is your fantasy.

> Nella is a real girl I really loved.
> My daughter.

Your one-time foster-daughter.
If your love is real you'll let her go.

In the event, I have written the letter and sealed the envelope, but not posted it. For the moment, that seems to be enough. The letter represents a mediation between the latent and the actual. By that, I don't mean the words I've written, which are prosaic. I mean the buff envelope enclosing the wafer of a message; the licked gum; the name decisively written in my round script, Ms Eleanor Franks. I carefully place the stamped addressed envelope in another envelope addressed to Mrs Jones at Shirehall, and shut it away in my desk drawer, definite but dormant.

Already they have strung up Christmas lights along the main road, plunging us into the year's end before we've properly acclimatised to autumn. On Remembrance Day, Catherine and I, with Dorothy and Nathan, join a second detachment of the Peace Group in the alternative wreath-laying at the Quarry. Next year, it has been suggested to the British Legion, the white poppyists might be allowed, in all reverence and respect, to join the red poppyists at the Remembrance Service. The Legion has replied to the effect that this will happen over their dead bodies. They don't want the ritual to be politicised.

'It's all about people, not politics, they say,' reports Hannah from chapel.

'People are politics though, aren't they,' Dorothy

argues. 'I mean, everything we do is a political action. Or don't do.'

'Exactly,' says Nathan hoarsely. He is shivering with cold, despite the mildness of the day, and, though he seems rather weak, insists on standing, which Cathy and I ensure by supporting him at either side. 'We must fight . . .' he begins.

'I don't hold with the word "fight",' objects a powerfully built elderly man, whose dignified posture reminds one of a retired Wing Commander. 'It isn't a term we ought to be using. That's their language. We must think of terminology without military connotations, and stick to it *upon all occasions*.'

' "Struggle"?' suggests Nathan, accepting the rebuke.

Apparently that won't do either. Too aggressive; suggests wrestling or rugby, equal anathemas.

'How about "oppose"?'

No, too confrontational. We must have a language of peace.

'Oh, come on,' says a dissident voice. 'You can't censor half the dictionary. Nothing would ever get done.'

A brief and courteous but impassioned wrangle breaks out amongst our party of pacifists, over the legitimacy of any combative terminology. After some strife, it is agreed that Nathan might in conscience fall back on the word 'work', but by this time he has forgotten his sentence.

The Last Post and Reveille have sounded.

The airmen from RAF Shawbury, the soldiers from the Yeomanry, the Mayor of Shrewsbury and Atcham in tricorn hat, the councillors in bowlers, the old soldiers and war-widows, the standard-bearers in white gauntlets, the company of rememberers, have all departed.

'I didn't like to say it,' confides Catherine as we

wander off together in the direction of St Julian's, 'but I'm not sure if I'm a pacifist at all. I mean, if someone were to attack my children, I wouldn't work, or even struggle, I'd *fight*.'

The white poppy on my breast covers up my violent heart.

I change the subject; swerving it away from where May cowers before my onslaught.

Through the passage, beneath the dark holly-arch, we make our way into St Julian's Church. All hell resounds within, as the thunder of hammer-blows pounding on metal echoes to the roof: a blacksmith? a cobbler or carpenter? This place stupefies me. It seems to sum up all we've come down to. The disused church has become a craft centre, where commerce transacts itself in an arcade of bustling booths, between the monumental pillars and beneath the ornate white ceiling of the once sacred building. Teddy-bears and chopping-boards, home-made millinery on a forest of poles, woodwork, slate-work, framing, dresses, beadwork: we process toward the Holy of Holies, to the music of the cash-till, past the brass eagle nesting in the pulpit, next to a pillar marked 'Restaurant'. Where the altar had been and the celebrant raised the host, and I once as a young woman wandering in off the streets, had knelt to pray for blessing on my forthcoming marriage, now Needle-crafts is positioned, and a woman selling candles with no buyers looks out with mild offence.

Cathy is enthusiastic; buys some soft leather shoes at the cobbler's, lincoln green. She says it's so good that we're keeping the old crafts alive. Oh look, what's this? Isn't it beautiful? Look at this, Jessie, do. I keep my mouldy sentiments to myself; mull over the spinning loom, the printers' calligraphy samples, with their text for the day: 'If you like it, buy it; please don't copy out.'

Who is that woman, hovering around the beadwork? I'm sure I recognise her.

'Hello,' she says. 'Do you remember me? I'm Stephanie. You met me in the spring, I think it was in the Square . . . we had a nice chat.'

'I do recognise you,' I say vaguely. The cobbler resumes his cobbling, with tremendous clangour. 'I can't quite place . . .'

A tall, earnest-looking woman in a green coat, with shoulder-length brown hair, glasses and a backpack . . . it's embarrassing when you're caught like this . . . but, oh yes, it's the woman with the Ordnance Survey map.

'Of course,' I say, 'of course. How are you? . . . Pardon? – you can't hear yourself think in here. Why don't we go and have a cup of coffee in the Restaurant? Cathy, this is . . .'

Pop music blares within the wood-panelled walls of what had presumably once been St Julian's vestry and now shares in the general desecration, with a cheerful grotesquerie. We wedge ourselves into pews covered with frilly cushions, view bunches of onions hanging from the wall, and savour an air of profanity and odour of spice. My eye is rendered distraught by the busy design on the plastic tablecloth, with its fruitarian design of apples, plums and peaches. Two Italian waiters alarm a pair of visitors by shouting the names of all the kinds of cake on offer at the tops of their voices.

'Scones, we'll just have scones, please.'

This austere choice arouses disapproval. But our order for tea, and just tea, and nothing but tea, plummets us to the bottom of the hierarchy of patrons. In this pandemonium, I ask the visitor how she's faring.

'Oh, yes – pretty good, thanks. I'm managing great

on my own.' Has made Shrewsbury a home from home, and rents a terraced house overlooking the river in Longden Coleham for occasional breaks. 'I love it here,' she says.

'That's right,' I recall. 'You were saying how different it is here from Manchester.'

'Right,' says the woman. She is consumed by delight at the multiplicity of charity shops and insists on doing a roll-call and head-count. 'That's at least twelve. It's so caring and unspoilt here – a kind of innocence.'

'In the eye of the beholder?' I enquire, rather astringently. Catherine flashes me a sidelong look of enquiry. I never used to give vent to caustic cracks. I used to be so nice.

It makes her feel my pain, Catherine has told me, when she hears the raw edge to my voice nowadays. It makes her long to help heal the wound – but she can't, and she knows she can't; and last week, when I snatched a glimpse of her swooping down on Joe in the supermarket, where he'd been screeching in his trolley, and hoisting him high in the air, making the laugh leap between them from face to close face, I'd been unable to stay; I'd left without a word, all scorching, minus my purchases, thinking of Nella, of Jacob, of Sebastian, knotted inside by that sense of exclusion that dogs my bad days like a jeering companion.

'Well, I expect you're right,' concedes the woman. 'Inevitably, mine is an outsider's view.'